Welcome

continue the vegan lifestyle, but if I never ate another banana again, it would be too soon.

It was at this time I found Dr. McDougall and his diet *The Starch Solution*. I thought, Hey, I love potatoes and rice. I can do this! And I did. Over the next six months I lost forty pounds without any effort. I rarely exercised, and I ate as much as I wanted. It almost seemed too easy.

Now it has been over two years on my weight-loss journey, and I've learned a lot along the way. I dove into every plant-based book I could find, and even got my certificate in plant-based nutrition from Cornell University. I love learning and using my body as an experiment (in a way) to see what truly worked and what didn't.

In those two years, leading up to today, I believe I have found the ideal diet for overall health and effortless weight loss. I have lost seventy pounds, and I've found my ideal body weight while eating as much as I want. Now I'm here to share with you exactly what works and bypass what doesn't to get you to your dream body in the most straightforward way possible.

The LEAN & CLEAN guide gives you fourteen days of meals, tons of information, an exercise plan, shopping lists, and motivational tips to kick-start your new healthy plant-based life. It is designed to help you build good habits with food, exercise, and the relationship you have with your body. The focus is on whole foods because those are the most health-giving foods on the planet. Whole starches, vegetables, lentils, fruits, and whole plant fats give our body the proper nutrients and energy so we can feel and look our best every day.

Over the next fourteen days, you can develop a balanced lifestyle that works for you. Don't worry, I will help you stay on track to achieve your goals after the jump-start is over, and you can always come back to it and re-create your own meal plan with the recipes and exercises you enjoy the most.

I have found what people struggle with the most is just that—getting started—so this guide was written to help you build strong habits and develop a positive mindset while mentoring you every step of your journey to the best health imaginable and the body of your dreams.

LEAN & CLEAN is flexible by design. You can switch around any of the meals to fit your schedule. You will find base meals with optional add-ons so you can get as creative or basic with your food, depending on your mood or your time. Living the whole food plant-based lifestyle is meant to be fun, but it's also meant to be easy, quick, and stress-free.

This guide is full of information so you have the knowledge you need to tackle everything from the naysayers who ask consistently, "Where do you get your protein?" all the way to making informed decisions about what to eat while traveling, natural beauty tips, and an exercise program to fit your individual needs and preferences.

The way to follow this program is to take it day to day, which is the successful way to do anything in life. Am I right? One step at a time. One foot in front of the other. You know the deal. We need to keep moving forward at our own pace, and as long as we're pointed in the right direction, we will get to where we want to go. I hope you are ready to live your life in a whole new way because today is the first day of the rest of your life. Let's get started!

Welcome!

Welcome to LEAN & CLEAN. My name is Hannah, and the first thing I want you to know about me is that I can relate to you in so many ways. I believe you are reading this book because you want to get healthy, shed weight, and start living the life you deserve. I'm here to help you.

I have struggled with my weight throughout my entire life. I remember going on my first diet when I was twelve and in the sixth grade. I ate nothing except carrot sticks all day long with small portions of what my parents cooked for dinner because I thought the less I ate, the thinner I would become. I would lay in my bed at night and do sit-ups and calisthenics until my muscles no longer moved. Looking back at that memory pains me. It marks the beginning of a lifetime struggle with my weight and body image, and to this day I pray no other person will ever have to go through the same struggle.

Over the next fifteen years my weight yo-yoed like crazy. I gained some here and lost some there, but I never understood how to eat healthy or care for my body. I starved myself for days before breaking down and eating everything in my house. This was my way of dieting, but it never got me anywhere. In fact, it led me to a very dark place where I no longer knew how to deal with the basic stresses of life.

Around age sixteen, I turned to drugs and alcohol to help me cope, which, as you can guess, made things a whole lot worse. By the time I was twenty years old, I was smoking a pack of cigarettes a day and drinking one to two bottles of wine a night while "sticking" to the low-carb diet that never got me anywhere. I knew I had to change, but I didn't know how. I searched for inspiration, which I found online through social media.

When I was twenty-seven years old, I decided to go vegan—raw vegan. There were a few people on YouTube and Instagram who talked about how they ate tons of fruit all day, felt energetic, and lost weight. In my eyes, they were living the dream. Eat as much as you want? No way! This was when my life changed for the better. I decided this was it. I would quit smoking, quit drinking, and become a raw vegan. I started out by eating thirty bananas a day because that's what I was told to do. People said I needed to eat tons of food because raw fruits and vegetables will cure everything and you will never get fat from eating them.

I ate around 3,000 calories a day and, to make a long story short, I gained weight—thirty pounds! The eat-as-much-fruit-as-you-can life didn't make me feel very good after a while. I became more depressed over time (particularly due to weight gain), felt lethargic, had the worst acne of my life, and I was always hungry. In the summer of 2014, I decided I couldn't eat this way anymore. But I was grateful I found this lifestyle because even though I had gained weight, I overcame a lifetime addiction to cigarettes and alcohol. I knew I wanted to

Lean & Clean

THE ULTIMATE PLANT-BASED WEIGHT LOSS GUIDE

BY HANNAH JANISH

Table of Contents

WELCOME TO
Lean & Clean

Why Lean & Clean?

Since there are many ways to eat vegan, why would you want to follow a starch-based program? I have found a starch-based plan established on whole foods is the best in terms of satiety, cost, and it's the easiest to stick with over the long-term.

Starches are the foundation of human evolution. If you don't believe me, read Catching Fire by Richard Wrangham. No, not the Hunger Games book. Sorry. We evolved as humans by being able to grow, store, and cook starches. Think about it. If we never had come across the holy potato we would all still live in the tropics eating bananas, we never would have been able to populate the northern and colder climates because there would not have been any food! Starches have kept us healthy, energetic and lean for a long time. They are by far the healthiest foods on the planet because they provide us with filling, slow-digesting carbohydrates that fuel our active lives and keep us satisfied until our next meal. The eating plan within this guide is the closest to what the healthiest, trimmest, and most long-lived cultures on the planet eat day in and day out.

STARCH

In the pages to come, not only does the meal plan use lots of potatoes, rice, and legumes, but also lots of vegetables and fruit. A balanced whole food low-fat diet is the easiest for losing weight and keeping your sanity. You can eat until you're full every day. You never need to go to bed hungry. You can have wonderful foods to satisfy your taste buds. Because the foundation of these foods is starch, your blood sugar will remain stable, your digestion will work well, and you will have a much healthier mindset throughout your journey because you will feel satisfied. Not to mention, it's an inexpensive way to eat.

Through my trials and tribulations on losing weight on a vegan diet, I believe I never would have gotten my dream body if I had not eaten a starch-centered diet. I was never satisfied eating tons of fruit. It didn't work with my body, and it digested so fast I was left feeling hungry again an hour later after I ate a huge fruit meal. It was expensive and unrealistic for my life. I also had a full-time job so lugging around a dozen bananas with me every day was not only annoying, but I looked like I was crazy.

You're here because I'm guessing you've tried everything as well.

I'm here to teach you how to do this the right way and shed the fat you've carried around for years. We will do that by going back to the most basic diet of human evolution: The starch-based diet.

OKAY, BUT WHY IS THIS BOOK VEGAN?

Through our studies of scientific literature we have learned that a whole food plant-based diet works to keep us healthy and lean because it ensures a number of health benefits. It can also prevent and possibly reverse some of the most common diseases that kill hundreds of thousands of people per year, like heart disease and type 2 diabetes.

Veganism isn't just about the health of our bodies, it's also about the health of our planet. Up to 51% of global greenhouse gas emissions are due to livestock and their by-products. Raising animals as food uses about one third of the earth's fresh water. Eating one less pound of beef per year would save more water than skipping showers for the rest of your life. How crazy is that? Animal agriculture strips the planet of natural resources while polluting our air, waterways, and soil faster than we can imagine. It is responsible for 91% of the destruction of the Amazon rainforest that gives millions of animals and people shelter and food. If that doesn't shock you enough, imagine pulling 90 million tons of fish from the oceans each year. All of this is unnecessary because we do not need fish, meat, dairy, and other animal products to be healthy. We are, in fact, much healthier without them so we are destroying our planet for no reason.

1.5 acres of land can produce 375 pounds of meat or 37,000 pounds of plant foods for human consumption. That looks like the answer to world hunger right there. If we didn't use so much land to grow corn and feed for the six million animals we raise and slaughter each day, we could grow enough food to nourish and enrich the lives of 800 million starving people. That number means one out of nine people do not have enough food to live a healthy life. Think about nine of your close acquaintances and imagine one of them starving every single day and struggling to get enough nourishment for their body.

I know a lot of this may sound extreme, but

I am a big believer in karma. We cannot cause harm to another being and expect nothing bad to come from it. There is no such thing as "humane slaughter". Slaughter is slaughter, and you only think we're wrong about it because you've never seen the torture and pain the animals go through to end up on your plate. If someone hurt your dog or an animal you are close to, you would feel the same about hurting animals, right? Cows, chickens, pigs, and other farm animals are held in horrific conditions from the moment they are born until the day they are electrically prodded off a truck and their throats are slit. These animals are not treated with care and respect. They are a commodity, a dollar sign, and money in someone's pocket. Every time you buy cheese, meat, fish, milk, fowl, or eggs, you are paying these people to abuse and kill animals because you would never be able to do it yourself.

A vegan diet isn't just about you. It is about what is best for all beings and the health and future of our planet Earth. I want to take a minute to thank you. I want to thank you for deciding to live a life of compassion, and I want to thank you for waking up to the cruel and inhumane practices that happen every day and your decision to do what is best for all life on our earth.

More Resources

BOOKS	MOVIES
The Starch Solution	Forks Over Knives
The Pleasure Trap	Cowspiracy
The End of Overeating	Earthlings
The China Study	Speciesism
Prevent & Reverse	Vegucated
Heart Disease	Live & Let Live
How Not To Die	

How Did I Get Here?

So you ever sit around and wonder, "How did I get like this? How did I let my health and body get so out of control?" What you need to realize is it's not your fault, and you are not alone.

People around the globe are fatter and sicker than ever, and our normal remedy is to dive into the diet pills and go on a juice cleanse or a low-carb diet. Why? Because we all love a quick fix, and there are companies out there spending billions of dollars to advertise their magical weight-loss products to us. The fact is there is no quick fix, and most of us know why we have gotten to a place of ill health and excess weight. It's due to the food we eat and the exercise bike in the corner that's covered in dust or used as a clothes rack.

A lot of us may have been on a path to health for years and still remain overweight and frustrated. Many people still find it hard to lose weight and get healthy even when they eat a healthy diet.

WHY IS THAT?

Because you're going about it the wrong way, and I know this from my own personal experience. I gained thirty pounds when I first went vegan, and I'll tell you exactly why. I replaced my bad habits of drinking, smoking, and partying, and started binging. I may have quit all those terrible life-sucking habits, but gaining another thirty pounds by eating massive amounts of fruit and dumping sugar into my smoothies didn't help my cause. It hurt when everyone around me said, "I thought vegans were supposed to be skinny? Wow! If that's what happens when you go vegan, I'm never going to try that!" It hurt to gain so much weight, and it hurt because I felt like I wasn't a true voice for the animals. Who would want to follow in my footsteps?

That's what everyone told me at the time. "Carbs won't make you fat!" I'm not going to sit here and tell you they won't because I know from personal experience it can and does happen—to a lot of people.

If you eat the right carbohydrates and the right amount of them for your personal lifestyle, carbs will not make you fat. If you force-feed yourself massive amounts of food and eat a lot of processed carbohydrates like sugar, carbs will make you gain weight because their caloric density is so high.

If someone eats an Atkins-style diet of 2,000 calories a day versus someone who eats a high-carb low-fat vegan diet of 2,000 calories a day, the leaner and healthier person will be the plant-based dieter. The reason people lose so much weight on Atkins, Paleo, and other carb-restricted diets is because they are so low in

> Over the course of the next fourteen days, you will learn the fast track to plant-based weight loss and health.

calories, not because they are low in carbs. The average calorie consumption is about 1,200 a day or less on those plans, which is only doable because the diet makes you sick.

You can lose a lot of weight on a plant-based diet, and it is much easier than all the other fad diets because you will eat more. The calorie density of plant foods is so low, you can eat four to five times the volume versus a low-carb diet with the same number of calories.

It took me a lot of trial and error to lose seventy pounds and to get where I am today. You, my friend, are in luck because you don't have to go through the same experimentation that I did because I've already figured out what works best. Over the course of the next fourteen days, you will learn the fast track to plant-based weight loss and health.

Are you ready?

Why You Are

OVERWEIGHT & WHAT TO DO ABOUT IT

People who are bigger than others eat more. There is a multitude of scientific evidence that proves the less we eat, the less we weigh. Why can't we stop eating though? Why are some of us better at eating less while some of us put on weight to a point where it ruins not only our health but also our life?

Here's the good news. It's not because you are lazy or lack willpower. It's not your fault at all. In the last few hundred years, we have taken food and turned it in to a drug. Once you understand you are overweight because you are addicted to unhealthy foods, you can overcome this addiction by going back to our natural diet, which will return you to your natural weight.

This is possible. I have done it myself. When I first went vegan I thought meat, dairy, eggs, and other animal products were the reason I was fat. It was a huge part of what got me to that point, but even vegan foods are often filled with fat, sugar, and salt, making us unhealthy and overweight.

A lot of people lose weight in stages when they adopt a healthier diet. First, they cut out animal products and lose twenty pounds. Then they cut out processed vegan foods and lose another ten pounds. They cut out oil and lose more weight. After they cut out gluten or soy, they get closer and closer to a healthier diet and their natural weight. Doing all of these at once will fast-track your weight loss.

Our body is a sophisticated system that wants to remain in a state of homeostasis, a state of stable equilibrium. Our blood pressure, water levels, and the amount of oxygen we breathe are precisely controlled. We don't regulate how much air we breathe every minute on our own and, believe it or not, the same process is involved when it comes to our weight. The caveat is we must eat the right diet.

True, you can grit your teeth and force yourself to consume fewer calories than you need and go to the gym for two hours a day, but this never lasts and is absolute insanity. Our bodies, when given the right food, will automatically go to our ideal body weight. It is not in the best interest for our health to be in a state where we have excess weight because it does not positively influence our chances of survival.

When we are overweight, we can and need to eat as much as we desire because it is the only way to lose weight in the long-term. The problem is we artificially stimulate our appetites, which causes us to desire an unnatural amount of food. When we eat a whole foods plant-based diet free of salt, oil, and sugar, our appetites go back to normal and we desire the amount of food intended to reach the weight where our body can maintain optimal health.

A lot of people ask, "If I'm eating as much

as I desire, how will I lose weight?" Since we know it requires an energy deficit to lose weight, this is a puzzling question. But the answer is simple. When we are overweight, our body naturally turns down the intensity of our hunger drive and we desire less food. Once we reach an optimal weight, our hunger drive goes back to normal. This is why you cannot look at how much food another person eats and mimic their portions for your success. You need a different amount of food, and your body will tell you exactly how much that is by how hungry you get.

This is an intricate process within the body. If we exercise more, our hunger drive goes up. If we lounge around more, our hunger drive goes down. You do not need to worry about overeating because it is nearly impossible to overeat on a diet comprised of whole natural foods without added appetite-stimulating substances, like sugar, oil, and salt. Once you eat this way, you will realize how easy it is for you to intuitively eat. The food doesn't have the same drug-like effect when in its natural state. Of course, it still tastes good. But after you've eaten enough, your desire to eat those substances will become nonexistent until your body needs more fuel.

Sugar, oil, and salt not only makes our food taste better, making us want to eat more, they also give us a dopamine rush, making us feel good and wanting to eat more. The more we eat salt, oil, and sugar, the more our body craves salt, oil, and sugar. This is why we feel

hungry many times throughout our day. But if someone offered you a banana or some plain brown rice, you would turn up your nose. You're not actually hungry. You are craving something sugary, oily, or salty. This is why we need to remove these substances from our diet. Once we begin to eat real foods, we appreciate how they actually taste.

You may think the food in this program is bland in the beginning. It can take about fourteen-thirty days to adjust to our natural diet. Once you get through the first fourteen days, you will notice how sweet fruit is, you will notice the small amounts of salt in spinach and greens, and you will become satisfied from these foods. You may start to prefer them over the chemical-laden manufactured foods.

An interesting concept to understand is the palatability of food. Food manufacturers know this, which is why the most decadent, delicious, and addicting foods have the trifecta of salt, oil, and sugar in them. Ice cream or pizza, anyone? Palatability is not only how good a food tastes, but also how motivated we are to seek out that food. When a food item has a high salt, oil, or sugar content, we know it engages the pleasure centers in our brain in an irregular way, and it is overly stimulating and delicious. The thing people don't realize is the more you get used to eating these foods, the less and less delicious they become.

WHY IS THAT?

Because we get used to it in the same way you get used to the smell of someone's house.

> Sugar, oil, and salt not only makes our food taste better, making us want to eat more, they also give us a dopamine rush, making us feel good and wanting to eat more.

When you first arrive at a new friend's house, you may think it smells different or funny. Stay a few hours and you get used to it. Spend enough time there and you will no longer think it smells any different than your own house. We quickly conform and adapt to our environments so eating highly salted and decadent foods over and over again won't just cause an expanded waistline and major health issues, it also becomes less enjoyable over time.

Remember: The reason we continue to eat these foods over and over again is because we are so used to the artificial enjoyment of these foods that normal plant foods taste bland to us.

You will enjoy food for the natural flavors it has, I promise. Fourteen days is typically all it takes to reset your taste buds.

If you want to get to your body's natural weight and state of health you should eat this way as long as you can until you get there. Once you get to your goal weight, you will have more wiggle room when eating out or if you want a little salt, oil, and sugar on your foods from time to time. It will take time to get there. But the longer you eat this way, the less you will enjoy eating processed foods. Believe it or not, you will prefer your foods in their natural form.

The 4 Basic Principles
OF THE LEAN & CLEAN LIFESTYLE

WHOLE PLANT FOODS

That means all whole plant foods. Yes, you can have avocados. Hallelujah! The foundation of this program is a starch-centered whole foods diet. The calorie basis of your food is around 50% whole starches, 20% vegetables and greens, 20% fruits, and the last 10% is made up of whole plant fats like avocado, nuts, and seeds. With an easy-to-follow meal plan, including a shopping guide and weekly meal prep, you will whip together healthy meals in no time.

NO ADDITIVES

What's better than eating whole plant foods is enjoying them in their natural state without flavor enhancers like salt, sugar, and oil. All the recipes in this book use the natural flavors in whole plant foods, herbs, and spices. Trust me, the food is good!

DAILY MOVEMENT

Yes, you have to exercise. No, it's not like training for an Ironman competition. Daily movement is the key to building healthy habits, along with strong bones, muscles, and maintaining a healthy metabolism. The easy-to-follow exercise plan within this guide is one anyone can do regardless of your financial situation or current fitness level.

A POSITIVE MINDSET

Get your mind on the right track. This is the most important part of the book and program. The truth is, the biggest problem isn't knowing what to do, it's consistently doing it every day until you reach your goals.

No, this plan doesn't have a million rules. These four guidelines are all you need to get your health and body in its optimal condition. Fourteen days of following this jump-start will give you the foundation and motivation to keep going until you reach your goals.

The Most Important

PART OF THIS BOOK

I've shared a lot about my personal weight loss journey in this book, and there is a good reason for that. What I found is the more I studied myself, along with the problems I encountered along the way, the more I understood you and what you're going through. One vitally important thing for you to understand is this:

Education is not teaching people what they do not know. Education is teaching, showing, and leading people to behave as they do not behave.

Knowing and doing are two different things. You already know most of what I'm going to share with you in this book. You know if you eat healthy and exercise consistently day in and day out, you will lose weight. It's not the knowing we struggle with, it's the doing.

Reading this book will not make you lose weight, but understanding and applying what is in this book will get you that dream body.

You must understand what you want, and go out and act upon it every single day!

Many people think it's hard and a struggle to eat healthy and exercise, but it isn't. It is only you, thinking it takes incredible willpower or determination to get what you want, who keeps you away from it. We need to do it regardless of how much your old habits and thoughts want to hold you back. You have to bust through that shell and do what you have to do.

THAT'S IT?

Yes, that is it. You must act upon the desires you want and visualize how you want your life to be in your mind every single day.

You bought this book because you want something. You have a dream of a better body, to fit into your size 2 jeans, to have impeccable health, to strut your stuff down the street with incredible confidence knowing you are drop-dead gorgeous. Every so often that dream floats to the conscious part of your mind, and most of the time when this happens you push it away and think, "I can't do that. I'll never look like that. I've tried a million times." Or you think, "This is too hard. I am destined to be fat." You can do it if you know how.

You cannot escape a prison if you don't know you're in one. To some degree, we are all in a prison. We let our mind block us from what we truly want because we doubt ourselves and make excuses for why we can't have what we want.

We let our dream of having what we want float away so we never accomplish it. We might tell ourselves we didn't want it. It was just a pipe dream, and we go on living our lives in a mediocre state, convincing ourselves we are happy without it.

Ralph Waldo Emerson said, "Do the thing, and you'll get the energy to do the thing."

Say it aloud to yourself right now. Yes, out loud. I am doing this. I can do this.

DID YOU SAY IT? GOOD. NOW YOU'RE ON THE RIGHT TRACK.

A lot of people look up to YouTubers like myself and think I am this super-driven person who is capable of doing things beyond what they can do themselves, that I never mess up, but that is far beyond the truth. I am like you. I struggled for over two years to lose those seventy pounds. Looking back at my journey, I made it 100 times harder than it ever had to be.

WHY DID I DO THAT?

I didn't know what I was doing. You may have heard this before, but for every action, there is an equal and opposite reaction. Every single time I doubted myself or looked in the mirror and thought I wasn't good enough, that I was fat, that I had so much farther to go, that is what I got.

There were times in my journey when I was motivated, especially in the beginning. Whenever I was positive and ate healthy and worked out, when I kept the vision of my dream body in my head, I got the results I wanted. It was only when I thought, "This is so hard. I can't do this. I'm a failure," that I would eat junk food and sit around all day depressed.

There is no reason to doubt yourself. Ever. As long as you keep moving in the direction of your goal, you will get there.

One thing I want you to understand is this: If you put in a little effort, you will only get a little bit of results. If you give this program your absolute everything and keep pushing yourself toward your dream body, you will get it.

> We self-destruct ourselves with our thoughts first. What happens after those thoughts are actions that correspond with the negative vibration of that energy.

If you want to sit around and complain about how fat your thighs are and how you can't stop binging or eating junk food, that is about the only thing you will ever get. Energy flows where attention goes, and we put more energy into thinking about the things we do not want opposed to the things we do want. As stated above, every action has an equal and opposite reaction.

Think about how your life would change if you thought about the things you want 24/7. That fit lean body, vibrant energy, and health. Glowing skin, lots of friends, happiness, laughter, and good times. A life full of abundance.

That is what is waiting for you. You have to put your energy into thinking about it and start acting upon it. Here is where most people go wrong. They think about the life they want and feel bad about their current circumstances. Do you know where that leads them? Right back to where they started.

Think about the times when you eat unhealthy, binge, or lay around all day like a bum. What are you thinking when you do these things? You are not thinking about how excited you are to be healthy and fit.

You are thinking about how much your life sucks, maybe how this person wronged you, how you're not good enough, thin enough, etc. We self-destruct ourselves with our thoughts first. What happens after those thoughts are actions that correspond with the negative vibration of that energy.

Now think about when you were successful at something. I know when I thought about how excited I was to fit into my skinny jeans, have my dream body, and look healthy and vibrant,

The Important Stuff

my actions directly reacted to those thoughts.

I got out every day and exercised, I craved healthy foods, and I had the mindset of someone who was healthy, vibrant, and fit, and acted in a way that manifested it in my life.

This section outlines a step-by-step guide about how to get yourself in the right mindset to achieve your goals. Without the right mindset, your goals will be much harder to attain.

WE ALL KNOW WHAT WE NEED TO DO. THE PROBLEM IS, WE DON'T DO IT.

The biggest thing you need to achieve your goals is consistent motivation and drive to keep you moving in the right direction. We need to get this part down first. Believe it or not, eating and exercising are easy by comparison.

The Mind of a Fit
AND HEALTHY PERSON

Order is the first law in the process of creation because it gives you an understanding of your beginning and where you are going. Movement is the action we need to commit to no matter what. Detours or roadblocks will try to derail our efforts in getting to where we want to go, but we must keep moving.

When you have these two things working in your life, a pattern of growth begins to develop. This is how you move away from your current circumstances to the life you want to live.

HOW DO WE DO THAT?

When most people set out to accomplish a goal, they have their destination in mind, but they do not think of the entire picture. They don't think of the journey. Success is not a destination. Success is a journey. Success is not something you get. Success is something you become. You are not going to get a great body and that's it, that's all, this whole thing is over. You will become a healthy and fit person. It never ends, which is a good thing because you will have this success forever.

Change does not happen through forcing ourselves to eat healthy and exercise. Change happens when we truly want to eat healthy and exercise by adopting the mindset and thoughts that we would have if we were already where we wanted to be.

You've heard the saying, "You become what you think about." Now you might think this is not true, but I promise you it is a fact. Mindset is not something anyone ever teaches us to do, so most of us do not think in a way which is to our advantage. We don't think good things most of the time, especially when we think about ourselves.

The most successful people on this planet think good things about themselves. They move in and around this world in a confident manner. They are confident because of their positive thinking. Instead of thinking, "I'm stupid. I'm so fat, and I'm a lazy bum," successful people think, "I am driven. I am smart. I am amazing."

We're taught it is bad to think about ourselves like this. We're taught that thinking good things like this makes us stuck-up or full of ourselves, but it doesn't. It makes us stronger because we become all the good things we think about.

I want you to run through a day in your mind and think of the most common things you say to yourself.

What do you think about yourself when you wake up, walk to the bathroom, and look in the mirror? What do you think about yourself while you eat breakfast? What do you think about yourself while you work out?

Positive thinking is a skill which benefits our lives instead of destroying it. What is required in order to think effectively? Entertain this idea for a second. When you think about something, do you think in pictures? Take a second and think about someone in your life who you love. Picture them in your mind interacting with you, like a movie. This is the basis of visualization.

When we visualize things or think about them, we start the process of creation. This happens because during this process, we evoke an emotional response to how that thought makes us feel. You visualize all day every day, whether you think you do or not, and your life is a re-creation of what you visualize the most.

Take a second and think again about that person you love. Imagine going up to them and giving them a long hug. How did that thought make you feel? Did it make you feel good?

Thinking about things is the basis of creating things in your life. But it's not the thought that creates movement. It is the emotion, the feeling the thought created within us.

Emotion = *Energy in Motion*

We have a lot of crazy thoughts during the day, but most of them don't create any impact in our life because they do not have any emotion behind them. They don't have any power. It was a random thought. But the most powerful thoughts create movement in our life, which is what will help us attain our goals.

When people think negative thoughts, they often create a feeling of depression, sadness, defeat, etc. The reason people fail when they try to change their life is because they are stuck with negative thoughts about themselves, which leads them to engage in activities that will continue to make them feel bad.

What happens when we feel depressed? We give up. In your health and weight-loss journey this will throw you off track. When you get frustrated and throw everything out the window and reach for the pizza, beer, and ice cream, it's when you think thoughts like "I'm a failure. I'm not strong enough, and this is too hard." And what happens the next day? You feel bad for failing, again, and you say, "Today is a new day. I'm going to change my life. I can do this." You motivate yourself again and start all over. It's a terrible cycle. The key is to control our thoughts so we never give the negative thoughts a chance to throw us off track.

Thinking is an activity and our body is the manifestation of that activity. Your brain is comprised of hundreds of thousands of cells. In these cells, we create pictures through our thinking. When most people think of their body, they picture images of poor health. They think about how fat their thighs are or how they have floppy arms and a pudgy stomach. We always focus on the things we hate the most, which is the opposite of what we want to do.

The goal you want to accomplish is to take and build the recognition of cells in your brain for a healthy and fit you. You can do that through repeating positive ideas about ourselves over and over and over until you build a different pattern of thinking. You are going to think and feel as if you were already at your goal weight. That might sound crazy, but I promise you—it works like magic.

You need to understand that your body responds to your thoughts. A lot of people think food is an evil thing that makes us fat. That's not true. It's the way you think about it that makes it true for you. As long as we eat the right foods, which we will learn about in the second part of this book, we will be healthy and maintain our bodies' ideal weight.

So, the first thing you need to realize is food is just food. It is here to give our bodies nourishment and energy so we can go about our lives doing the activities we want to do.

The lack of having a fit lean body and good health only exists when we make room for that idea in our mind. What does that mean? It means our thinking and focusing on the lack of what we do not have brings that lack closer to us. You are overweight and unhealthy because you think you are overweight and unhealthy. It is a part of your consciousness that you have brought to you through your negative thoughts.

Being healthy and fit is a mindset. If you are not healthy and fit, it's because you have the mindset of an unhealthy and overweight person.

DOES THAT MAKE SENSE?

I know that whenever I saw a girl walking down the road with a perfect body I thought, "How does she do it?" Or I thought, "How does she have all this drive to exercise and eat healthy while it's such a struggle for me?"

It was a struggle because my thoughts held me back. I thought it was a difficult thing to prepare healthy foods. I thought exercise was torture. I thought I was unmotivated and lazy, but none of that was true. My new habits began when I shifted my thinking.

Once I realized food was good for me and I needed it to have energy and to keep me healthy, I was no longer afraid of it. I stopped craving processed vegan junk food because it was no longer something forbidden or bad for me, but something that didn't provide me with the energy and nourishment I craved.

When I no longer looked at exercise as torture, but thought of it as a way to build my strength and health, I sought it out and looked forward to it every day. I lost weight, looking better and feeling marvelous, which propelled me to keep going.

This is the mindset of a healthy and fit person, the mindset you will learn to adopt. You can do anything you want to do in your life, but you have to get out of your own way.

The number one thing that you need to accomplish your goals is to have a positive mindset about yourself. As Theodore Roosevelt said, "Believe you can and you're halfway there."

You are your biggest motivator. Learning how to think properly will give you the drive to keep you going no matter what you want to do. Every single day when you think something about yourself, I want you to make a conscious effort to make those thoughts positive. This is hard for many people in the beginning. But I promise you, this is one of the most life-changing things you can do.

We want to push out the negative and destructive thoughts with good thoughts to keep you motivated and moving in the direction of your goals.

You may have negative thoughts in the beginning, and that's okay. The fact that you realized you had a negative thought is more than most people will ever do. When you have that thought, replace it with something positive. If you think, "I am lazy," flip it around and think instead, "I am strong." Don't only think the words, but think of all the reasons you are strong. Think of your past accomplishments and things that prove to you that you are a strong person. You need to feel emotion behind your thinking. Emotion is energy in motion, so do anything in your power to make yourself feel proud, beautiful, strong, etc.

Remember: Learning is not gathering information and doing nothing with it. Learning is when you consciously entertain an idea, get emotionally involved in the idea, which causes you to step out and act on the idea. That will, in turn, improve the results in your life.

Think Thin

This program will not work for you until you have established a goal. A goal is something that you are emotionally involved in and working to accomplish.

"You must know WHAT you want, WHY you want it, WHEN you want it, and have an idea of HOW you're going to get it." - Napoleon Hill

In this next section, you will write down your goal. This goal is not about how much weight you want to lose. It's not about what size jeans you want to fit into or your dream measurements.

Think about how you want to feel about yourself when you get healthy and lose weight. How will you feel when you are at your goal weight or fit into those jeans? Write it out in the present tense.

I feel beautiful. I love how I feel in my clothing and how everything fits me perfectly. I feel strong and healthy. I feel confident when I talk to people. I am always happy and smiling.

Writing out this goal should give you chills. You should get excited when you read it, and that excitement is what will motivate you to follow the path to achieve it.

Write this goal on a piece of paper or in the notepad in your phone where you will see it each day. I made my goal the background for the lock screen on my phone and read it as much as possible. That is what you want to do.

Read your goal as much as possible. When you read it, feel the feelings of having it now. Think about this: What will it take for you to feel beautiful, confident, and sexy?

The answer is nothing. And there is no reason for you not to feel that way now.

Your self-perception and how you see yourself is important. How you constantly feel about yourself is what you attract back to yourself. Confident, beautiful, sexy people know they are what they think of themselves, and they reflect that image because it is how they feel about themselves at every moment.

People who are unhealthy, depressed, feel fat, ugly, lazy, or whatever label you want to put on it, go through their day thinking bad things about themselves so they continue to experience those feelings day in and day out in their life.

You may think I'm crazy to say you need to feel, act, and think the way you want to see yourself, but that is exactly what you need to do. It isn't an easy thing to do because you have thought a different way your entire life, but this is vitally important.

When we think, act, and feel the way we want to be when we reach our goal weight, those acts are what propel us to do what is necessary to get there. It isn't difficult because it feels like we are already there.

Thinking, acting, and feeling like you're already at your goal does two things. It keeps

your conscious mind on track with what you want to accomplish by reinstating it in your mind as much as possible. You know where you are going and what you want to achieve, and this keeps you on a definite path to get there. It also gets you into the state of mind or vibration to receive your goal and make it happen. When you feel good, excited, happy, you are on the same level as your goal and it isn't a struggle to keep going. It's exciting.

We struggle so much with achieving what we want when we are rarely excited or happy about the journey we are on to achieving that goal. We think more in a state of lack. We don't have what we want and we feel bad about not having it, which pushes us farther away from it. We need to be excited about the fact that we are in the process of receiving it. You are on the path to your goal and every single day you get closer to it. Get excited! That is how you will achieve it. Results come to you in this manner.

> ## Thoughts + Feelings + Actions = Results

Your thoughts make up your mind about what you want, your feelings express your desire that you have about what you want, your actions are the movements that propel you through the created excitement to achieve what you want, and the results are the manifestation of those actions. To change your results, change your thoughts, feelings, and actions.

Once we learn to change our thoughts, feelings, and actions, we develop habits. Everything we do is the result of the habits formed during our life, and our habits are the main reason we remain the way we are in our current state. Only through changing these habits can we see results.

Thinking negative things like, "I'm so lazy. My thighs are so fat. I hate healthy food," gives you those results. No one walks around believing they love eating healthy and exercising every day while eating fast food and sitting in front of the television for hours. Every time you think about these things, you give them more strength and these thoughts take up more space in your subconscious mind. So, wouldn't you want to think positive things that will help you realize your goals?

Your habits are fixed ideas in your subconscious mind. Once this happens they no longer require any thoughts to cause us to act on them.

Consciously observe some of the things you do in any given day. Stop, watch your own behavior, and listen to your thoughts. What you will find is many of the things you do are done through habit. You automatically do things you don't want to do that give you the results you currently have because of your formed habits.

WE KNOW WHAT WE ARE SUPPOSED TO DO, WE JUST DON'T DO IT.

Why don't we do it? It's because the habits we have are subconsciously keeping us from what we truly want.

Write down three habits you want to create. Every single day throughout this program think thoughts that will manifest those ideas. Here is an example.

HABITS

- I work out every day for thirty minutes.
- I eat healthy and make my own food every day.
- I read my goal of how I want to feel every morning and go throughout my day feeling as if I already have it.

THOUGHTS

- I love getting outside and moving my body. Working out makes me feel energized, fit and healthy. I love the energy I get after doing cardio exercises.
- I love the simple taste of fresh fruits and vegetables. I crave healthy food because it gives my body the nutrition and energy I need. I love spending the time to make fresh meals when I know what is in them.
- I am beautiful, and I love taking care of myself. I have glowing skin and eyes. I love how I can make people laugh. I love feeling confident and sexy.

If you do this exercise, you will start to feel good. See how that works together? Think good positive loving thoughts to feel good. Think destructive negative bad thoughts to feel bad. The key is to feel good! Do anything in your power to make yourself feel as great as you can each day.

Some people will see that and say, "Well, that's great, Hannah, but I have depression. I can't feel good." Depressed feelings are the result of negative thoughts. Once you are consciously aware of your thoughts, I guarantee you that you will want to think good things most of the time.

Go through your day and think good, positive things that will lead you to form these habits. Feel proud of yourself when you do this because you are accomplishing something most people never learn to do.

The rest of the program is worthless without this basic understanding. You have the mental ability and the power to change your life, and now you have the understanding of how to direct it. By practicing this, happiness, health, and prosperity will manifest in your life, and it should because that is your birthright.

DO THESE THREE THINGS BEFORE YOU MOVE ON TO THE NEXT CHAPTER.

1 Write the vision for your life in the present tense in your notepad, journal, phone, etc. You can start by saying, "I am so happy and grateful now since…" and how it makes you feel now that these things are present in your life. You can follow this up with thinking about how certain things smell, feel, taste, sound, or look.

Dive deep in to the details and the more real you can make this vision for you, the quicker it will become real in your life.

"I am so happy and grateful now because I feel so beautiful. I love how I feel in my clothing and how everything fits me perfectly. I feel so strong and healthy. I feel confident when I talk to people."

2 Write out three positive health-building habits you want to introduce into your life. Follow this up with the positive thoughts you will think as a result of those habits.

3 Have your notepad, journal, or phone close by when you wake up each morning. Spend two minutes going over your vision and habits. This will remind you of them. Spend five to ten minutes in a relaxed state and visualize what you wrote down in step one. Listen to your favorite type of music that puts you in a good frame of mind. Remember: Focus on the feeling. Visualization is meant to be fun and exciting.

"Right now you are looking at the results of your past creations and right now how you feel is creating your future." - Odille Rault

Starch Versus Raw Vegan

Why isn't this diet revolved around eating raw? A lot of people ask me that question, and a lot of times I get comments that fruit is tastier and easier to eat. But the thing is, it is not nearly as satisfying as cooked starches.

A million years ago, we evolved by including cooked food into our diet. As you may have noticed, we are not chimpanzees. Our stomach is about one third the size of the average chimp and they chew close to six hours a day. The average human chews about one hour a day. The time reduction in chewing, the size of our stomachs, and the strength of our jaws are not designed to eat 100% raw food diet. Our diets have gotten softer as time went on, meaning we ate more cooked foods in each decade.

Human nature was born behind the advent of fire. Fire is the singular tool that changed the course of human evolution.

Over a million years ago, protohumans, Australopithecus, had no long-term mating relationships between the male and female, meaning there were no families. There was a standard operating procedure, which is true for 97% of mammals on the planet, where the male had no paternal investment in the offspring whatsoever. He did his thing in the woods with a female and went along his merry way. The females had the children, were in charge of them, and they fed and raised those children for many years. When you have children, there is no way that you can hunt while protecting your children at the same time.

Our early ancestors evolved as a raw food species. Neither the male nor female hunted and both ate the same food, primarily fruits and leaves, which are abundant in the tropics. Keep in mind this was way back before we had the ability to speak. Our species was like any other animal.

Then something extraordinary happened. Around this time, one million years ago, fire was discovered and was used to cook food.

Women cooked root vegetables, which are much higher in calories than eating fruit or leaves off the vine. They couldn't eat these tubers raw because they weren't palpable. It took too much energy to eat and digest them without cooking them first. Once we learned to cook them, they became much softer and made them easier to digest, which gave us more energy.

An odyssey began when women collected root vegetables during the day and cooked them each night to eat and feed their children. The problem was there was no way to stop male humans from coming in and stealing all their food. The men were stronger and were able to swoop in, once the women were done cooking, and run off with everything. Other animals stayed away because they were afraid of fire. Their instincts told them fire meant danger. In their world, a forest fire meant they would die. Human beings were able to use fire to intimidate other animals away from them, but humans were not afraid because they used fire as well. Males sat around and waited for some poor female with children to light a fire and cook all her starches before he swooped in and stole all their food, and there was nothing she could do about this.

What happened next is how we formed relationships within our species. The dawn of pair-bonding happened when a male paired himself with a female and said, "Hey, I'll stand around and protect you and your three children as long as you feed me." Now when the thief came around the corner, he saw a woman with her children cooking food with a man there holding a spear, protecting the food.

This evolved into villages of ten, twenty, or thirty men, women, and children with a bunch of fires cooking food. We evolved as a species when we developed relationships and ate cooked food. It is also how we were able to collect starches, and grow them ourselves using farming. We inhabited not only the tropics, but the colder climates as well.

Think about it like this. Where does the majority of fruit grow year-round? The answer to that is in the tropics and closest to the equator where the temperatures are warmer. We never would have been able to inhabit the planet and evolve as a species if we weren't designed to eat cooked food.

Without the use of fire and the ability to cook root vegetables, we would have remained in the tropics and would still be there today. We'd spend about six hours a day eating and another six hours searching and gathering food.

Through time humans evolved by eating more and more cooked food. Why is this? We wanted to increase our chances of survival. That means we wanted the largest number of calories for the least amount of work, and it's how we evolved to survive.

At this point in human evolution we are at a terrible place because our environment is filled with foods that are highly stimulating, dense in calories and low in nutrition. Consequently, as a whole, we are getting fat, sick, and riddled with diseases by eating these manufactured foods.

To be healthy and lean and not just survive, but thrive, we need to go back to our natural diet, which is whole plant foods. Starches, vegetables, legumes, fruits, and whole plant fats.

Raw food diets are difficult to maintain. A lot of raw food advocates try to mimic the calorie density of cooked foods. They do a lot of dehydrating, blending, and processing of their foods. This makes it easier to consume a larger number of calories from foods that are normally low in caloric density.

I'm not saying that a raw food diet is unhealthy because it is 1,000 times healthier than what the majority of the world eats, but it is difficult to feel fully satisfied on raw foods. It is often a struggle to afford the quantity of good quality fruits required to make it work in this day and age.

In our hearts and stomachs, we crave 500 calories per pound of cooked foods. Potatoes, rice, squashes, carrots, and other whole starches are what we thrive on. Throw in some fruits, greens, non-starchy vegetables, and a little bit of nuts and seeds, and we have an all-around appropriate diet for the current evolution of our species.

Why You're Fat
AND YOUR FRIEND ISN'T

We all have one of these friends. It looks like they eat any amount of junk food and don't have any weight issues. It's frustrating when they stay slim despite eating calorie-dense foods, but you can't lose any weight despite trying every diet program under the sun. What's going on here?

ONE THING WE NEED TO UNDERSTAND: THE LAW OF SATIETY.

The law of satiety says animals in their natural habitat eating their natural diet will neither eat too much nor too little for their best health. We all have this satiety mechanism that regulates how much we eat. It is what regulates our hunger drive.

Think of it like this. The average adult woman over a twenty-five-year period, from age twenty to forty-five, gains an average twenty-five pounds. That's one pound per year. One pound of fat is approximately 3,500 calories. Dividing that by 365 days means the average women is overeating by about ten calories per day. Since the average person eats somewhere between 1,500-2,500 calories, it means they're systematically overeating by less than one percent of their total calories.

By looking at the last example, our satiety mechanism works almost perfect, but it is often fooled by processed foods that are unnaturally dense in calories.

So if you and your friend eat the same type of Standard American Diet, why are they slim and you're not? It comes down to the genetic variance in the number of our nutrient receptors in our stomach.

We all have two different types of receptors that give information to regulate our hunger drive. They are called the stretch and nutrient receptors. The stretch receptors respond to how physically full you are. For example, if you ate one pound of salad greens, physically it is a lot of food so you feel full, but it isn't a lot of calories.

One pound of salad greens is about 100 calories. Because the average human eats three to five pounds of food per day, that's only 300 to 500 calories a day. You won't survive on that low number of calories, and that's where our nutrient receptors come in to play.

If you ate 300 to 500 calories from greens per day, yes, you'd feel full, but you'd still be hungry because your nutrient receptors calculated that you only ate a small number of calories. The nutrient receptors calculate the approximate energy from your food by detecting the protein, carbohydrate, and fat amounts of the food you're eating.

This is important because there is genetic variability between you and your slim friend. Your friend has an abnormally high number of nutrient receptors, which detect the calorie

density of processed foods much easier.

Here's how this works. For example, let's say you and your friend both have a plate full of whole natural foods that equals 500 calories. It could be a combination of rice, beans, and lettuce. You both eat the plate of food, and at the end of the meal you both feel full and satisfied. Everything here is normal.

Now let's say that instead of whole natural foods, you both eat 500 calories of food from McDonald's. Food which is high in processed ingredients, salt, oil, and sugar. This food is calorically dense, more so than those whole natural foods.

Now when your friend eats the McDonald's meal, their stretch receptors aren't activated because the calorie density of the food is high while the volume of food is small. Their nutrient receptors will detect that the food is high in calories. It recognizes this and shuts off the hunger drive after they eat those 500 calories. They now feel full and satiated.

Now when you eat that same 500 calorie meal at McDonald's, your nutrient receptors aren't able to detect the calories as well and your body thinks it has only eaten about 400 calories. This is important because your hunger drive doesn't shut off because you're 100 calories short of 500, where you'd normally feel satiated.

So when you leave McDonald's, you're still ravenous and you grab one of their apple pies which totals 100 calories, and now you're at 500 calories. After you eat the pie, you feel satiated and your hunger drive is cut off. The problem is you have consumed 600 calories, not 500, which means you have systematically overeaten.

The caloric density of these unnatural processed foods throws off our ability to correctly assess the amount of energy we are getting from these foods. Your friend with the increased number of nutrient receptors is considered abnormal, and he or she is less likely to overeat on these processed junk foods because they can detect and assess the calories in these foods much easier.

The problem here isn't that you need to eat under your hunger drive, but you need to start eating the foods you were designed to eat in their natural state so your body can assess the correct amount of energy you are getting from it. When you do this, your body will naturally move to your ideal weight for biological reasons.

Your satiety system works perfectly normal, but you just need to eat the right foods from the time you're hungry until you're full. Once you do that, you'll find yourself slimmer and healthier than your friend in no time.

Why Calorie Restriction
DOESN'T WORK

Calorie counting. Why doesn't it work? To be honest, it does work. If you eat less than your body needs, you will lose weight. That's a fact. The problem is it's almost impossible to do this. Sure, maybe you can do it for a day, maybe even a week. Some people grit their teeth and impose this self-induced starvation to get to their goals, but it's impossible for most of the population.

There is a reason why you eat as much food as you eat. The average adult eats between three to five pounds of food per day, and the reason we eat that much food per day is because we have sophisticated hunger drive mechanisms inside of our brain. What these mechanisms do is drive us to eat X amount of food per day as we learned in the last chapter, *Why You're Fat and Your Friend Isn't.*

We know we have many stretch and nutrient receptors within our stomach that calculate our food and calorie intake. They are there for a reason!

Our natural diet of whole plant foods is perfectly designed to fill up our stomachs with the correct number of calories. The stretch and nutrient receptors need a specific number of calories and nutrients per bite to satisfy our homeostatic drive.

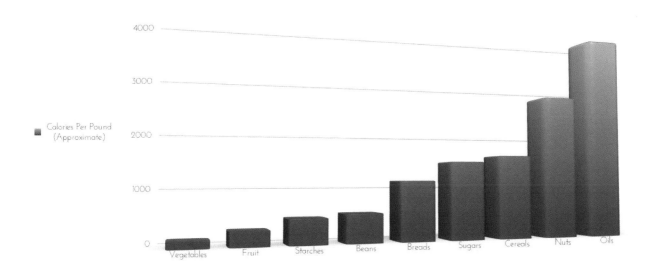

If we are eating the right food, we will eat about 400 to 500 calories per pound of food and we will be full and satisfied. Most people who try to lose weight in today's world will eat a 300-calorie bagel with cream cheese, a tiny cobb salad for lunch, and a lean cuisine 500-calorie microwave dinner. But there isn't any bulk when eating like this. Where is all the fiber and nutrients we need to satiate our homeostatic drive? All we have is a bunch of salt-laced refined carbohydrates sweetened with sugar and added fat.

WHAT THIS DOES IS MAKES US EVEN HUNGRIER, SO WE BINGE.

Dr. Doug Lisle compares this to sitting in a cold room with a sweater next to you but you're not supposed to put it on. Your brain is going to repeatedly tell you, "I should put the sweater on, I should put the sweater on, I should put the sweater on." You won't do it because you think keeping it off is going to help you in some way. This is called, "losing your mind," and people do it every single day when they are trying to lose weight. When you restrict your caloric intake, your body keeps telling you, "Eat, eat, eat, eat, eat, eat," and it takes tremendous self-discipline to lose weight this way or sustain the weight lost.

This is an unnatural way to go about losing weight. No animal in their right mind would ever impose this type of self-starvation on themselves and they don't need to because every animal in its natural habitat eating its natural diet is their perfect body weight.

WE NEED TO DO THE SAME.

When we eat a LEAN & CLEAN diet full of whole starches, vegetables, fruits, and greens with a little bit of whole fats, we satisfy the nutrient and stretch receptors in our stomach. We can then feel full and satisfied.

We need to eat as much as our body desires. As long as we are eating the right foods, that are not overly stimulating, and we give it time, we will return to our bodies natural weight.

Food Addictions

Have you ever met someone that was addicted to eating kale? What about plain boiled potatoes? I haven't. Usually people that say they can binge on whole natural foods are really just hungry. There is a difference. Food addiction doesn't make any sense as a general concept but processed food addiction does. Our bodies and our minds have motivational mechanisms that are designed to motivate us to do good things for our biology.

When we get thirsty, it doesn't happen by accident. We get thirsty because our body was in a state of dehydration and it needed replenishment. Our body sends a signal through our hypothalamus gland that is translated into a sense of thirst to motivate us to drink some fluids. No one is addicted to drinking water. Once you reach a good satiation point and have quenched your thirst, you are done.

The problem with food addiction arises when we start changing things within our food and making the stimulation artificial. It's not the food that you are addicted to, but it's the reaction you get from eating that food which addicts you to it. No one raids the fridge in the middle of the night to binge on a bag of celery.

That never happens. It's always the processed food, with an unnatural concentration of oil, sugar, and salt, we seek.

It's not addiction in a sense because no one goes through withdrawal symptoms when they stop eating chicken nuggets. It's hard to get away from eating chicken nuggets because frustration and a craving process happens, and they happen for a reason. When we eat these overly processed foods crammed with artificially concentrated fats, salt, and sugar, we get rewarded for eating those.

Think about winning the jackpot on a slot machine, when lights and sounds go crazy. That's what it is like in our brains when we eat these rich, artificial foods. We are rewarded with a dopamine rush from these foods. Some people relate it to a drug addiction.

In the next few chapters you will see why there is no oil, processed sugar, and added salt in the LEAN & CLEAN lifestyle, and how these three food additives cause your weight problems.

Dietary Thermogenesis

& DE NOVO LIPOGENESIS

Perhaps you have not seen these two terms before, but they are important in understanding weight loss when it comes to the macronutrient complexity of foods. A high-carb vegan lifestyle is the easiest way to lose body fat and maintain that loss, but why? It's due to the two terms above.

WHAT IS DIETARY THERMOGENESIS?

Also known as the thermic effect of food, dietary thermogenesis, or diet-induced thermogenesis, DIT, is the process of energy production in the body caused directly by the metabolizing of food consumed. Dietary thermogenesis is influenced by factors relating to the composition of the food and the physical state of the individual. A 2004 analysis published in "Nutrition and Metabolism" of research on dietary thermogenesis found that in an energy-balanced state, a mixed diet of proteins, fats, and carbohydrates produced an energy expenditure from dietary thermogenesis that constituted five to fifteen percent of total daily energy expenditure.

After you eat complex carbohydrates, like rice, potatoes, and beans, your body digests them into simple sugars in the intestines where they are absorbed into the bloodstream and transported to your cells and used for energy. If you overeat carbohydrates, the excess calories are invisibly stored in the muscles and liver as glycogen. Your body stores about two pounds of glycogen. If you eat beyond the limit of glycogen that your body can store, it is burned off as heat. That process is called "facultative dietary thermogenesis" because it's used in physical movements like fidgeting—not exercise.

> Converting sugars to fat is done through a process called de novo lipogenesis, which is the conversion of excess carbohydrates into lipids for storage.

Converting sugars to fat is done through a process called de novo lipogenesis, which is the conversion of excess carbohydrates into lipids for storage. Animals like pigs and cows can easily turn the carbohydrates from grains and grasses into fat, but us humans can't do this as efficiently. When this occurs, the metabolic cost is about 30% of the calories consumed, which is not only wasteful but inefficient. Say you eat an extreme excess of food, 1,000 calories over your daily limit. You will burn off about 300 of those calories in the process of fat conversion.

A few hundred excess calories will not get stored as fat as long as they are carbohydrate molecules, but 1,000 extra calories from carbs? In cases where people overeat, the body converts excess carbs into fat. And yes, you can get fat from this! I gained thirty pounds by doing this exact thing. The problem is, it's hard to overeat by thousands of calories day in and day out unless your food is full of stimulants like sugar, salt, or oil.

During the time I was gaining weight, I ate a lot of added sugar, concentrated foods like dates, huge 10-15 banana smoothies, and I also added salt to my foods. You do not need to worry about that on the LEAN & CLEAN lifestyle because you will naturally eat the right amount of food each day because we eliminate all stimulating substances.

If that didn't convince you, here's more food for thought. There are over two million species of animals on planet earth, but only three species currently have problems with excess weight. Do you have any guess what those three may be? Dogs, cats and humans. Don't you think it's a little suspicious that all of them live in human households?

This phenomenon is because a universal law is at work all the time, just as gravity works one hundred percent of the time and you don't see pigs flying around. It's called the law of satiety.

Animals that eat to satisfaction, also known as satiety, in their natural habitat will, over time, neither eat too much or too little for optimum health.

People see that statement above and say,

"That doesn't apply to us anymore because we don't live in our natural habitat."

That is true, we do not, but we do have our natural diet available to us to eat at all times. The problem is we don't eat our natural diet, which is whole starches, fruits, vegetables, greens, plus a small number of nuts and seeds.

Anyone I know who has eaten a whole foods plant-based diet consistently gets to his or her natural weight. The amount of time it takes them may differ due to many factors, but it always happens one hundred percent of the time. The reason we run into issues eating this way is because our biochemistry is firing on all signals, warning us against it.

We are programed to do three things: Seek out food, reproduce, and conserve energy. The reason we enjoy, crave, and seek out unhealthy and overly processed foods is because they give us a huge calorie hit for little effort. In nature we would seek out the foods which have the most calories with the least amount of work because that is how we ensure the survival of our species. What kinds of foods are abundant in our current habitat that have a huge calorie hit? Processed, packaged cookies, chips, TV dinners, fast food, and convenience foods.

The food companies know this. They know the easier food is to eat, the more likely it is to sell. Only about one tenth of the food in grocery stores is fresh produce, potatoes, rice, or other healthy whole plant foods. The rest is the vast selection you see throughout the aisles and aisles of packaged and processed "convenience" foods. We are far more likely to choose going through

> In nature we would seek out the foods which have the most calories with the least amount of work because that is how we ensure the survival of our species.

the McDonald's drive-thru versus going home and baking a pan of oil-free potatoes because our natural instinct is to conserve energy.

One thing you need to realize is our food is manipulated in a way that aligns with our natural desire for survival. We have to go against what our brain tells us to do to stay healthy in our current environment. We need to proactively choose to cook our own foods rather than choosing the quick, cheap, and easy route which leads us to disease and obesity.

I recommend reading the book *The Pleasure Trap* by Dr. Alan Goldhamer and Dr. Doug Lisle.

It explains in-depth the evolutionary psychology of why we have gotten ourselves in to such an unhealthy state.

Remember: The only thing we need to do is to eat whole plant foods. This is simple, and we need to make that decision over and over again to reprogram our brains and taste buds to crave our natural healthy diet as our humans once did long ago.

Oil - The Worst Food
FOR WEIGHT LOSS

Oil is not a food and it's definitely not a health food. Oil was once a component of food and it is in nearly every single plant food. That's not an issue when it's in its whole natural state because it is in the correct ratios for our body to digest, with the proper amount of water, fiber, sugar, minerals, and other phytonutrients contained within that food.

The problem arises when we extract the oil from our foods and pour it all over everything. It's now a concentrated fat, and our bodies love concentrated calorie sources. We get a lot of pleasure out of eating fatty, calorie-rich foods. But when these foods have been processed into oil we run into problems, not only with our waistlines, but also with our health.

OIL IS ONE HUNDRED PERCENT FAT.

There are 4,000 calories per pound in oil, which is nearly ten times more calories than in starches. Not only is it high in calories, but the concentrated nature of oil makes it easy to store in the body as excess fat. It also ends up on our skin.

Oily skin promotes bacteria growth that can cause severe problems with acne, which is particularly a problem for young people and teenagers. Oil is not included in the LEAN & CLEAN lifestyle because it isn't a clean food and it will not make you lean. That means any and all oil. Olive, flax, coconut, hemp, canola—all of it!

There are a lot of companies out there with deep pockets that will tell you all about the

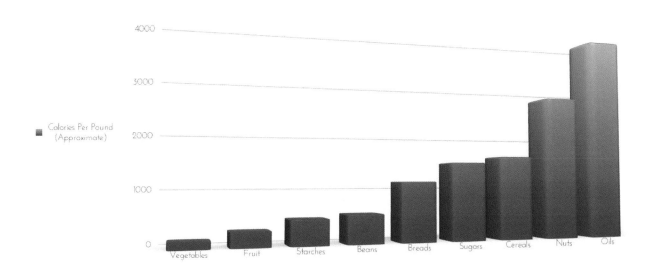

"health benefits" of oil. Any of these benefits are much better received by eating the whole plant itself. The only time you should use oil is for your skin or to fix a creaky door hinge. Got it?

Research has shown that people can eat as much of foods ranging between 300-400 calories per pound or less without gaining weight. People can consume relatively large portions of foods between 500-800 calories per pound and still lose or maintain weight, depending on their individual activity levels and metabolism.

The LEAN & CLEAN lifestyle is successful because you can eat as much as you want as long as you eat the right foods. Even a little bit of oil can set your weight loss back because you will consume a huge number of calories in a small amount. There is no nutrition contained within oil. At room temperature, oil is a liquid. If you freeze it, it looks almost identical to body fat. Oil contains 9 calories per gram, which means it contains more than twice the number of calories per gram than carbohydrates, making it the most calorically dense food found in nature.

If you are trying to lose weight, oil is one of the worst foods you can consume which is why it is not part of the LEAN & CLEAN *lifestyle.*

Whole plant fats like avocado, hemp seeds, flax, and sesame seeds are allowed because these foods are healthy for us and satiate us more than condensed sources of fat. I don't want you to think all fat is bad for you because whole plant fats are great for your body. They help to regulate your hormones, keep you more satisfied, and give you glowing skin, hair, and nails. I've found a lot of people who come to a high-carb vegan diet think that they need to cut out all fat and they think all fat is evil. When they cut out all fat from their diets, they end up with a lot of issues. They start losing their hair, their periods, their skin becomes dry, and they sometimes even become depressed.

Fat is good for you as long as you get it from the right sources.

> If you are trying to lose weight, oil is one of the worst foods you can consume which is why it is not part of the Lean & Clean lifestyle.

The
Spice Hunter®

DILL WEED

100% ORGANIC

*Your source
for true flavor.*

NET WT. 0.5 oz (14g)

THRIVE
—MARKET—
GROUND CINNAMON
ORGANIC | NON-GMO

2.24 OZ (63.5G)

SPROUTS
FARMERS MARKET

organic

Vanilla
extract

NET WT 2 FL OZ (59 mL)

Za'atar
SPICE BLEND

Net Wt. 2 oz / 57 g

simply
Organic.

turmeric

NET WT. 2.38 OZ. (67g)

Harissa
SPICE BLEND

Net Wt. 2 oz / 57 g

simply season

TRADER JOE'S
Spices of the World

French
Thyme

NET WT. 0.7 OZ (20G)

teaspoon

Why No Salt?

This book is intended to be 100 percent salt-free. With that said, I know salt is the hardest thing for people to give up. I know it makes food taste ten times better, but if your goal is to lose weight you will become more successful without it, or at least minimizing it as much as possible from your diet. On the other hand, the most important thing is to eat the right foods.

Many people are not at a place in their journey where they want to give up salt, and that is okay. If you have just gone vegan or are starting your weight-loss and health journey it may not be critical to give it up right away. Will you get faster results if you do? Yes, you will see major changes much quicker. But we want to suggest a program you can easily follow so if you feel like you need a little more flavor in your food, add a tiny amount, 1/8 tsp, to the surface of your meal before you eat it. Do not add any salt to your foods when you are cooking because the taste dissipates substantially and you still get all the sodium.

Another thing to try is a salt-free breakfast and lunch, but include a small amount of salt on your food at dinner time. This approach works to readjust your taste buds. If you have salt first thing in the morning, your brain will crave it all day, causing you to eat more. A little bit of salt goes a long way, and the sodium we need we can get from whole plant foods.

Do what feels right to you and work on enjoying foods in their whole natural form. This will get you to the healthiest and happiest place. If you need a little salt on your food, don't stress about it too much. You'll still get great results.

WHAT IS SALT?

Sodium is a natural salt is found in every single whole plant food in varying amounts because it is an electrolyte and 100 percent necessary for the health of our bodies. Usually when people think about salt, they think about table salt, sea salt, Himalayan salt, or any other kind of salt which has been chemically processed and packaged. This type of salt is not the same as what is found in natural whole plant foods. Sodium chloride is an inorganic salt our body does not recognize, seeing it as a toxin.

You probably know salt makes our bodies hold water, right? Some of you may have experienced this. After you eat too much salt, you can't take your rings off or your face suddenly looks puffy. The scary thing is salt holds more water in our artery walls, which makes them less elastic. This is why people who have high blood pressure are told to go on a low-sodium diet.

When people eliminate salt from their diet

> We need about 500 - 600 milligrams of sodium every day, and we can get all of that through whole plant foods.

they typically lose around five pounds of water weight because our bodies hold onto excess water as salt is toxic to us in high amounts. Whenever we consume salt we actually increase the toxic load on our bodies, and the only way for our bodies to cope with this toxin is to dilute it. Because we consume too much salt on everything we eat, our body is not able to rid itself of it.

Salt is a powerful appetite stimulant and it is also very addicting. Think of how many potatoes you can eat when you chop them up into fries, sprinkle them with salt, and dip them in ketchup. Now think about how many plain potatoes you could eat without any salt or ketchup. Salt makes food more interesting. It enhances the flavor of everything so the more salt in your food, the more food you will eat.

There are times when we are not even hungry, but we crave salt. This happens when the body sends us a signal to seek out something salty, but no one is going to eat plain salt, right? That would be disgusting.

What happens is we end up eating more food to get our fix, which is a huge reason we can't lose weight. When I first started eating salt-free, I made myself the same portions of food as I did before, but about halfway through my meal I lost the desire to continue eating. When my food was salted, I could easily eat all my food and go back for more!

We need about 500 to 600 milligrams of sodium every day, and we can get all of that through whole plant foods. Even though all plant foods have some sodium, if you find you are missing salt there are some with higher amounts, like greens, celery, vegetables, sea vegetables, and tomatoes. Feel free to include those in your daily diet.

Eating salt-free is the hardest part for people because our taste buds have adapted to salty foods. You will notice in the next few weeks that you will start to appreciate foods for how they taste in their natural form . When was the last time you had brown rice or a potato without salt and appreciated the food the way it was naturally intended?

It's crazy to me that people think these foods are boring in their whole natural state. The reason they think that is because they are addicted to salt. Trust me, potatoes, rice, corn, and beans all taste excellent without added salt once your taste buds adjust.

You may have cravings for salt in the next two weeks, but know it is a simple craving. It will go away. As long as you make sure you eat enough, you will overcome it and your taste buds will go back to the way they were always meant to be. It is much easier to lose weight when we do not chemically alter the flavors of our food with excess salt, sugar, and oil. You will be able eat as much as you want at every meal without any worries because it is nearly impossible to overeat this way.

Refined Sugars

What is so bad about maple syrup, coconut sugar, or molasses? Not a lot, honestly. These foods are healthy and they do not cause any harm to the body. The reason they are not allowed on the LEAN & CLEAN lifestyle is because they are overly stimulating and they are a very dense source of calories.

What we want to focus on in this program is eating whole foods that have all the fiber, water, minerals, and phytonutrients intact, because it is the quickest and healthiest way to get to our ideal weight. It's also easy to cook with whole plant foods, and you will discover during the next two weeks that you can easily sweeten your foods without refined sugars.

Instead of using refined sugars we use dates, mango, banana, and other whole natural fruits to sweeten our meals. Trust me, a bowl of oatmeal is satisfying with a bunch of fruit mixed in with it. You won't even miss your drizzle of maple syrup. A lot of people overeat because they add tons of jam, syrups, and sweeteners to their foods. I see people dipping fruit in coconut sugar all the time, and they wonder why they can't lose weight!

These sugars are a refined source of calories, which is great if you are at your ideal weight and need a lot of calories to power through a long distance run or bike ride, but it is not satiating to the stomach receptors in the same way whole plant sugar satisfies, like fruit. When we systematically overeat over and over again, it can make our weight loss frustrating and difficult.

If you are serious about shedding the extra pounds, give up the sugar. It doesn't have to be forever. These foods are okay, but save them for when you are at the point when you're maintaining your weight.

"Salt, sugar, and fat, combined with chemicals in processed foods, trick the brain in the same way as cocaine, and the brain flushes our bodies with dopamine, perhaps the most blissful, and addictive, homemade chemical we have. Once we find a way to trigger it, we kill ourselves to get more. Literally." - Dr. David Kessler

Why You Need To

GET OFF CAFFEINE

Most people don't realize how powerful caffeine is until they try to give it up. Let's be honest. If you drink coffee, it is probably the first thing you think about every morning after you pee. I was one of the biggest coffee drinkers before I started my health and weight-loss journey, and for the first two years of eating high carb low-fat vegan diet, I still drank coffee.

This section is how coffee and caffeine ruin your weight loss and fitness goals. We'll put aside all the touted benefits of it. You may stop and say, "Wait, Hannah, but coffee is healthy, look at this article I found online." Honestly, no offense to you, but I don't even have to read the article to know it is one-sided in favor of coffee, coffee producers worldwide, and a coffee company probably paid to have that research/article/blogpost written.

I'm not denying coffee may have possible health benefits, such as the antioxidants it contains. However, drinking coffee, caffeinated teas or other products with caffeine fries your adrenals over time. Caffeine stimulates our body to produce cortisol, elevating heart rate and blood pressure, which is why we get that "fight or flight" response. When this happens on a consistent basis, a decreased resistance to this stress occurs. Which means we develop a tolerance to it, just like we would to any other drug. If that wasn't bad enough, consuming caffeine on a daily basis causes your body to produce less dopamine and serotonin, which are 2 of the important feel-good hormones.

The human endocrine system is complex and drinking caffeine often messes up your hormones in a very big way, which is a huge no-no if you want to get fit, lean, and healthy.

Like I said before, caffeine is a drug, and it's addictive as hell. If you've ever tried to give it up before you will know what I am talking about. Caffeine withdrawal is terrible. If all of that wasn't enough to convince you to go caffeine free here's ten more quick facts for you. The caffeine in coffee increases catecholamines, known as stress hormones. These hormones respond by releasing cortisol, which can mean weight gain, aging, and increases insulin, which screws up your blood sugar levels.

While all of this is happening inflammation in the body occurs, which causes all kinds of problems. It could be something small, like slow recovery from workouts, trouble losing weight, acne and skin issues, to something big like fibromyalgia or multiple sclerosis.

Have you ever heard of insulin sensitivity? Insulin sensitivity is exactly what it sounds like. It is how sensitive your cells are to the effects of insulin. Low insulin sensitivity makes it difficult for your cells to respond appropriately to blood sugar. When your body is not properly regulating its blood sugar, especially on a high-carbohydrate, diet your energy levels will feel like a roller coaster. It can also be hard to stay satisfied with appropriate amounts of food because your blood sugar levels are all over the place. If you've ever felt like you were starving after eating 500 calories of potatoes or bananas, this is why.

Unfiltered coffee has the highest number of beneficial antioxidants, which is what all those articles online are about, yet also leaks the most diterpenes into your system. These diterpenes have been linked to higher levels of triglycerides than normal, along with higher LDL and VLDL levels. All bad news if you want to be healthy and fit.

Addiction is also an issue with coffee drinkers, and that addiction makes it difficult to rely on our body's natural source of energy. You start to habitually consume it everyday for a pick me up instead of eating something more nutritious that is going to give you real, long lasting energy and nutrition.

HOW DO I GIVE IT UP?

Cut back to one cup in the morning for a week, half a cup for the next week. Switch to green tea for another week and drink a herbal substitute like Dandy Blend or Teeccino after that. Once you get over the first thirty days, you won't miss it and you will feel better than ever.

I have so much more energy, and it lasts all day because I do not rely on a stimulant that messes with my mood and hormones. No more 5 pm headaches from the withdrawal, either. When I wake up, instead of making coffee I drink a liter of water with half a lemon squeezed into it, and I feel more energized and balanced than ever before, which gives me the energy to live my life to the fullest. If I ever have a craving for coffee I get a decaf or have a decaf chai tea with soy milk.

Most people find the flavor, smell, comfort, and habit comes from drinking something warm and familiar in the morning. Do the best you can. This may mean cutting back from four cups of coffee a day to one or drinking one to two cups a week instead of every day. Like I said before, most of these problems are from relying on caffeine every single day to pick you up and get you going. Having it once in a while is much better than every single day.

What You Need To
TO KNOW ABOUT GLUTEN

Gluten generally is not a problem for people unless they have a sensitivity to it or are allergic, also known as celiac disease. The problem is most people who are sensitive to gluten have no problems at all, so how do you know if you have a gluten allergy or just a sensitivity?

You can have a blood test done that will test you for celiac disease. You can also do an elimination diet where you consume a very, very strict diet for a few months, or you will notice different issues showing up in your daily life such as acne, skin rashes, migraines, joint issues, or even depression. It can be hard to distinguish if these issues are caused by gluten though which is what makes it so tricky. Its almost easier just to not eat it, or have it every once in a while. Nevertheless we are going to go over these one by one to reveal how gluten contributes to their cause.

ACNE

If you have had problems with acne and haven't been able to figure out why, gluten sensitivity might be the issue. Gluten can contribute to acne in a few ways. Acne is a result of blood sugar problems and typically this is coupled with inflammation as well. This causes hormonal reactions that lead to increased sebum production, blocked pores, and an overgrowth of acne-causing bacteria

or oil on the surface of your skin. Gluten can cause damage to the small intestine if you have a sensitivity to it. This can lead to nutritional deficiencies and an increased toxic body load, like leaky gut syndrome or IBS.

People with a gluten sensitivity cannot digest gluten as effectively as someone without it. Which means they do not completely absorb the digested protein molecules. What happens next is the immune system treats these undigested molecules as invaders. The body see's these invaders and responds by releasing histamine, which increases inflammation. Then the inflammation increases insulin resistance in the nearby cells which causes insulin resistance that we talked about in the chapter addressing caffeine. It's not the gluten that is causing acne, it is actually the insulin resistance that is causing it.

HEADACHES AND MIGRAINES

Food sensitivities are often widely known to cause headaches. A recent study showed that 56% of people diagnosed with migraine headaches had an underlying gluten sensitivity. After the subjects removed gluten from their diet and adopting a gluten-free lifestyle, their migraines diminished. If you have been eating a lot of products containing gluten and getting recurrent headaches, this could be your issue.

JOINT PAIN AND INFLAMMATION

As we talked about with acne, people who are gluten sensitive increase the inflammation in their body. Increased inflammation results in joint pain along with other aches and pains within the body. Animal products can also cause joint pain as they create excessive inflammation in the body. Getting rid of these 2 culprits in your diet will help you the most.

DEPRESSION

As I said before gluten can cause a leaky gut which disrupts your bodies ability to absorb certain nutrients like B vitamins, iron, vitamin D, and zinc. These nutrients are very important for your mood and health. If you decide to give up gluten, ensure you get your essential B12 and daily sun exposure to rebuild vitamin D. Studies have shown that multivitamins generally cause more harm than good so I always advise against taking them unless you have another condition that they help. We can get all of the nutrition our bodies need and in the correct amounts eating whole plant foods.

RELIEF

The way to relieve the issues caused by this stop consuming gluten. Luckily, this entire 14-day meal plan is gluten-free. I recommend sticking to gluten-free eating for these 14 days while taking note of any of the above issues if you ever had them in the past. See if they get better and when the 14 days are up, you can gradually introduce gluten back into your diet to see if you have flare-ups. If you do, you know for sure you are sensitive to gluten and will want to steer clear for the best health.

JUST A TIP: If you're sensitive to gluten you don't have to swear it off forever! Have it as a treat meal once in a while when going out or getting an epic vegan pizza.

All About Calcium

How weird is it we're brought up to believe that drinking the milk of another species is beneficial to our health? If you don't think that you've been brainwashed to drink cows milk, just think how bizarre it sounds to drink giraffe, cat, or horse milk.

WHY WOULD ANYONE WANT TO DO THAT?

We are meant to drink the milk from our mothers, just like a baby calf drinks the milk of its mother. A calf doesn't drink human milk right? Within the confines of a dairy farm cows are impregnated over and over so that they have a calf. The only way a cow can produce milk is if they have a baby that needs it, like humans. The calf is taken from the mother, sold for veal, and the milk is sold to humans.

It's a business and it is a business that has been fooling us all our entire lives. You don't need the milk from another animal to get calcium, just like you don't need the flesh of another animal to get protein. We can get all our calcium from plants.

Our bones contain large amounts of calcium, which helps to make them firm and rigid. Calcium is also needed for other tasks including nerve and muscle function and blood clotting. These tasks are so important for survival, that, when dietary calcium is too low, calcium will be lost from the bone and used for other critical functions.

Vegetable greens such as spinach, kale, broccoli, legumes and soybean products are great sources of calcium. An 8oz glass of soy milk has fewer calories, less saturated fat, less sodium, less sugar, and the same amount of calcium and protein as an 8oz glass of cow milk.

Studies have shown that vegetarians absorb and retain more calcium from foods than do non-vegetarians. The absorption rate of cow milk isn't high at all. In fact the western world has the highest rate of osteoporosis and we also have the highest consumption of dairy.

This is because people consuming dairy products excrete more calcium than they ingest. The animal proteins break down into types of amino acids, which leach calcium from the body. This can cause and worsen conditions like osteoporosis. American women have consumed an average of two pounds of milk per day for their entire lives, yet thirty million American women have osteoporosis. Drinking milk does not prevent bone loss. The most effective way to strengthen bones is exercise and a healthy plant-based diet.

As long as you're eating a well-rounded plant-based diet, there is no need to worry about calcium consumption. You are far better off getting your calcium from plant sources as the body absorbs it better. Spinach, kale, broccoli, and other whole plant foods do not contribute to disease or the harming of other animals and the planet.

SCARY FACTS
About Dairy

Got Pus?
The FDA allows 750 million pus cells in every gallon of milk

Disease
Dairy consumption has been linked to cancer, diabetes, autism, schizophrenia, and many auto immune diseases like multiple sclerosis

Osteoporosis
High dairy consumption means a higher rate of osteoporosis

Water
It takes 2,000 gallons of water to produce one gallon of cow milk

Cow Deaths
Dairy farms contribute to the slaughter of over 21 million dairy cows per year

Lactose
A whopping 75% of the population is lactose intolerant and most don't even know

Weird Humans
No other species on the planet consumes milk in their adulthood or consumes the milk of another species, except humans

But What About Protein?!

The one thing you will need to get ready to hear as a vegan is "*But where do you get your protein?*" The majority of people believe that we need tons of protein to function on a daily basis and that we can't be strong and healthy without meat and dairy. This is false. Have you ever met anyone with a protein deficiency? Anyone?

According to the American Dietetic Association, a plant-based diet supplies much more than the required protein for one's daily need. Harvard University researchers have found that it is practically impossible to eat a plant-based diet and produce a protein deficiency. Proteins consist of twenty different amino acids, eleven of which can be synthesized naturally by our bodies. The other nine are the essential amino acids. These must be ingested from the foods we eat. So the first eleven our bodies can make, and the remaining nine we must get from our foods. We do not have to get them from meat and dairy because they are naturally found in plant foods!

Here's how it works. The animal would eat the plants containing all these essential amino acids and then we would eat the animal to get our "protein," which doesn't make any sense. It's like taking your nutrients and filtering them through a sewer. Think about how much muscle a gorilla, hippo or rhino has and they are plant-eating animals. They all get their protein from plants and they are also some of the strongest animals on the planet. We are also plant eaters, we get our protein from starches, vegetables and fruits and we can get all the protein we need, minus the heart clogging saturated fats.

The "need" for high protein is centered on fear rather than fact. The initial research on which this myth is based was done in Germany around the turn of the century and was financed mainly by the meat and dairy industries. The average American consuming animal products, meat, dairy, eggs, eats more protein than he or she needs.

One example I like to give people is think about a human new born baby. They typically weigh around 6 pounds on average and after 1 year of their life, they are usually around 4-5x that size. The first year of our life is the fastest rate we will ever grow in their human life. When our bodies grow rapidly especially in our younger years adequate protein intake is essential. So think about his, what do human babies eat? Breast milk. If you look at human breast milk it is typically around 3% protein. Why would an adult, who is fully grown need more protein

> If you look at human breast milk it is typically around 3% protein. Why would an adult, who is fully grown need more protein than an infant? The answer is they don't!

than an infant? The answer is they don't! It is a myth and lie perpetuated by the meat and dairy industry. Even the World Health Organization says that we only need about 3 percent of our calories coming from protein to live a healthy long life.

High protein diets are dangerous! All that extra protein produces toxic by-products that the liver must process and before it is excreted by the kidneys. It also increases IGF-1. If you don't know what that is, it is insulin like growth factor. IGF-1 is very important in our growth during childhood but high levels of it in adulthood actually leads to the proliferation of cancer cells and metastasis of cancer.

The Hippocrates Health Institute showed that the people who ate the most meat were more susceptible to protein deficiency. First, the body finds it difficult to digest animal protein because it often doesn't get fully digested. Instead it putrefies in our intestines. Gross, right? Meat takes days to digest, but plants only take hours to digest completely.

The more excess protein there is in the diet, the more it problems it causes within the body and it can make it much harder, if not impossible to lose weight. As toxins and waste builds up in your system, you start to suffocate at a cellular level. The buildup of protein contributes to hypertension, atherosclerosis, cardiovascular disease, cancers, and diabetes. So when someone asks you where you get your protein, tell him or her you get it from the same place the animal they're eating gets it. *Plants.*

The Importance Of

GOOD DIGESTION

Good digestion is probably the most important thing when it comes to general health and weight loss. I know it's the last thing anyone wants to talk about, but we're going to talk about it now. I'd be lying if I said after I went whole food plant-based vegan everything became perfect. It took quite a bit of experimenting and trial and error for me to get to where I am today, but one of the biggest things I can tell you is digestive health is important.

We've all done terrible things to our bodies over the years by eating crappy diets, not exercising, taking over the counter drugs and antibiotics, drinking alcohol, and taking in other harmful substances. If we thought our body would become 100 percent healthy from eating a whole food plant-based diet for a few months, we were naive.

While the number one thing we can give our bodies is clean air, water, whole plant foods, exercise, and love, the next biggest thing we need to give it is time. It needs time to heal from everything we have done to it. The biggest healing takes place in our digestive system, and I don't just mean our stomachs. I mean our stomach, kidneys, liver, bowels, and every other part along the way.

Our digestive system does so much more than we realize. It breaks down food into fuel, amino acids, and hormones, but also gives us energy, regulates our mood, and gives our body the nutrition we need to live healthy lives.

A poorly functioning digestive system means you're unlikely to receive much nutrition from the food you eat. This will stimulate hunger, leading to weight gain, as well as general tiredness and that run-down feeling.

For the long-term, the health implications are much more serious. It is said that all disease starts in the gut. That may be hard to verify, but it's pretty clear that good health is difficult to obtain without good digestion.

Triphala is an ancient Ayurvedic preparation of three dried fruits, amalaki, bibhitaki and haritaki, with incredible body cleansing and rejuvenating properties.

Taken in a certain way and at a certain time, triphala is an effective digestive system cleanser. It gently clears away trapped waste products and toxic compounds. Most important triphala doesn't just clear out your system, it also nourishes and rejuvenates the membrane lining of the gastrointestinal tract.

> A poorly functioning digestive system means you're unlikely to receive much nutrition from the food you eat. This will stimulate hunger, leading to weight gain, as well as general tiredness and that run-down feeling.

Most people who start an effective cleanse by using triphala drop a few pounds in a short period of time from the amount of crap they clear out of their system. That's a good start, but in for the long-term a properly functioning digestive system means your body is getting the nutrients it needs easier so you won't feel hungry as often.

If your body has poor digestion and assimilation, you may eat a lot of food without getting the important minerals, vitamins, and other nutrients you need. Your body knows it requires these substances to operate effectively so it stimulates more hunger in an attempt to get them.

Through following the LEAN & CLEAN lifestyle you will be giving your body what it needs on a daily basis and in time your digestion will improve dramatically. Some people see results instantly when adopting a whole food plant-based diet but for others it can take a little bit longer.

Remember: If you have digestive issues, it is generally because of the food you have eaten prior to adopting a LEAN & CLEAN lifestyle. After years and years of fiber deficiency and eating foods lacking in nutrients, our digestion becomes weak. A lot of times when we eat whole plant-based foods with a lot of fiber, we encounter digestive disturbances until our system gets used to it and the proper gut flora and bacteria builds to properly digest.

Invest in a strong probiotic if you experience digestive issues in the beginning to get your system jump-started. You don't have to take this forever. It is only to help you grow proper gut flora in the beginning. The best brand I have found is Now Foods 25 billion probiotic. Taking this by itself or in conjunction with triphala will get you up and running in no time.

Your body needs time to adjust. I recommend supplements because I know how helpful they can be, especially when it comes to digestion. No one wants to be bloated and constipated while waiting for their system to reboot itself. These supplements are not necessary by any means.

After about two weeks on the LEAN & CLEAN lifestyle, you will have much better digestion. But if you want to help your digestion get into optimal condition, these are the supplements I recommend.

Now Foods Probiotic
https://highcarb.co/probiotic

Organic India Triphala
https://highcarb.co/triphala

Bloating & Constipation

Digestion involves the mixing of food, its movement through the digestive tract, and the chemical breakdown of the large molecules of food into smaller molecules. Digestion begins in the mouth, when we chew and swallow, and it is completed in the small intestine. The chemical process varies somewhat for different kinds of food.

Our intestines are muscles so when we come from eating a diet low in fiber, known as The Standard American Diet, restricting our calories, juice fasting, or even a healthy diet such as a raw food diet that is easier on digestion, our intestines become weak and worn out. Your gut flora adapts to the environment you give it so changing your diet means your gut needs time to adjust to the new foods and adapt to breaking them down properly.

Once you adopt a high-fiber starch-based diet, it can be common that you have a bit of bloating, constipation or gas that you may not have experienced much of before. Don't worry.

The main cause of this is weak stomach muscles, but your muscles will build strength to digest your food like a champ! The good thing about this is all you need to do to make your stomach muscles stronger is eat, how fun is that? No crazy gym workouts necessary. To be clear, we're talking about your intestines. Having six-pack abs won't help you digest brown rice. Sorry.

Now you may already have a strong digestive system and you won't have this issue. Remember: Healing takes time so sit back, be patient with your body, and eat.

Tips for Goood Digestion...

- **STAY HYDRATED.** Drink 1/2 - 1 liter of water before every meal, especially first thing in the morning. Adding some fresh squeezed lemon can also help.

- **MOVE.** Get outside every day and move your body for 30-60 minutes. If you have digestive issues or have not gone to the bathroom in a while, go for a long walk, jog, or bike ride.

- **STICK TO WHOLE FOODS.** Rice, potatoes, beans, corn, greens, vegetables, and fruit all in their whole forms. These foods have everything in tact and will not cause digestive disturbances or dehydration like flours or more processed ingredients will.

- **KEEP YOUR DIET LOW IN FAT.** 15% fat is ideal for women on this plan. Keeping refined fats like oil out of your diet will help your digestion move along much more efficiently. Higher fat foods will slow your digestion and clog you for a while because fats do not travel through the body as smoothly as clean carbohydrates.

If you have given these tips a shot for a few weeks and need something to help you … ahem … move things along, there is a natural herb called triphala, mentioned in the last chapter, that works wonders for people. It is not a laxative or stimulant in any way, but a rejuvenating and detoxifying herb popular in Ayurvedic medicine. It helps to cleanse and support your GI tract, improving the digestion, elimination, and the assimilation of nutrients. It also helps remove fatty deposits and toxins from the intestines and is rich in vitamin C and antioxidants.

I mention this herb because I know a lot of people that will say "screw it" and go out and buy laxatives or something unnecessary if they have issues. Those types of drugs will make the problem worse in the long run. Let's be honest, sometimes we need help with things like this. After years and years of feeding our bodies animal products and processed foods, it can take some time to reverse and heal the damage. I do not think using natural remedies is a cop-out, but it's up to you to determine if you need more help in that area.

Time will heal these kinds of ailments so relax and let your body do what it does naturally.

Consistency

One of the biggest things that will make or break your weight loss is consistency. Our bodies love it when we are consistent. Our bodies like it when we give them what they need and love it when we continue to do that in the future. Our metabolisms thrive when we give them the same amount of healthy plant-based foods every day, when we get outside and move, when we drink enough water, get enough sleep and have positive loving thoughts about ourselves. That's when our bodies know what to expect and begin to feel safe and cared for.

Most of us, come from backgrounds of yo-yo dieting, fasting, under eating, or a generally poor diet. Our bodies have never been truly taken care of before so they are not healthy and hold onto excess weight because who knows when we are going to start starving or eating low carb again. Look at the two calorie models to the right.

Option A is probably how you used to approach your diet. I know it's how I used to do things. I started every week on Monday and I always thought, "This week is going to be the week I change my life. I'm going to stick to it this time." I'd starve myself by eating as few calories as I could, about 1,200 or less, and exercise as much as possible. I would burn out within a few days, binge, and make up for it the next day by eating a ridiculously low number of calories, around 800, and binge again the next

A. STARVE & BINGE

	Calories	Exercise
Mon	1,200	no exercise
Tues	1,400	ran 6 miles
Wed	2,600	no exercise
Thurs	800	ran 3 miles
Fri	2,100	no exercise
Sat	1,300	no exercise
Sun	2,800	ran 9 miles

B. SLOW AND STEADY

	Calories	Exercise
Mon	1,800	30 min light cardio
Tues	1,800	60 min light cardio
Wed	1,800	30 min light cardio
Thurs	1,800	30 min light cardio
Fri	1,800	60 min light cardio
Sat	1,800	45 min light cardio
Sun	1,800	30 min light cardio

day. I repeated this cycle and never lost any weight in the process. Why? Because my body was confused. It didn't have any idea what if it was going to get fed so it held on to as much weight as possible. I never got in shape because I was never consistent with my exercise, and I was stuck in this cycle of starving and binging.

It is much better to eat more calories and do a little bit of exercise every day than to eat less.

Eating less isn't going to help you lose weight. You need to be satisfied with how much food you're eating or you'll end up back where you started.

THE BEST THING YOU CAN DO IS TO BE CONSISTENT.

Find an amount of food that satisfies you and eat about that same amount every day. Figure out how much exercise you can do every week. Enjoy it while you're doing it and do it every week. Go to bed at the same time every night. Keep your body properly hydrated, and make sure not to stress about your body and weight loss because it will come with time. When you stress about things, it makes it worse. Stress is one of the biggest causes for weight gain, acne, and depression so take care of yourself the best way you can, be consistent, and give it time. What we want to focus on is progress.

PROGRESS NOT PERFECTION.

Trust me, I didn't wake up one day, look in the mirror and love myself unconditionally. Just like I didn't love eating healthy food, exercising daily, and taking care of myself instantly. It took some time.

I had many, many bumps in the road, but every time I ate junk food, went out and partied with my friends or relapsed back into old habits, I learned something. I learned that I love feeling good.

I love to wake up in the morning, drink a big glass of water, do some yoga, make a healthy breakfast, and start my day. I never would have gotten to where I am today unless I screwed up all those times. I learned with every failure what I wanted, and I learned how not to screw up again.

You are not going to be 100 percent healthy and perfect all the time, and you don't need to be. You are going to binge, slip back into old habits, not get enough sleep, and eat junk food. It's going to happen, and it's okay!

Many people have expectations to rigorously follow a plan for the next six months without any slip-ups so they can have their dream body by their birthday. There is no time frame on health. It's a process, and our bodies are constantly changing. The key is to learn to change for the better. It's all about how you tackle the situations that come to you every day.

MAKING MISTAKES IS A PART OF LIFE. EVERYONE DOES IT. NO MATTER HOW PERFECT THEY LOOK.

The goal isn't to strive for perfection. It's about doing the best you can with your own goals and the circumstances you are given in your life. If you fall off the plan or have a bad day, the best way to handle this is to admit you made a mistake. I know it's never easy to admit this, especially to yourself, but it's a crucial step in learning, growing, and improving yourself.

You can only learn from a mistake after you admit to yourself that you've made it. If you say, "Oh, it's fine, I'll start again tomorrow." You never register in your brain that you did something you consciously didn't want to do so you never learn from it. It will always be a constant escape to repeat the action in the future because of the way it made you feel in the moment.

The first step is to replay what you did in your head. Say to yourself out loud in the mirror. "I know I made a mistake by " and state what you did. Afterward, smile and say to yourself, "I forgive myself, and I will use this opportunity not as a failure, but as a valuable way to better myself."

The next step is figuring out why you made the mistake in the first place. The best thing to do is to write this out in a journal. State what you did wrong and go through the sequence of events that led up to it. Answer these questions to yourself.

- How was I feeling in the moment?
- What benefit did I believe doing this action would cause me? - Did I have attainable goals set?
- What was the negative effect of this mistake?
- Were there multiple small mistakes that led to a larger one?

By answering these questions, you will not only uncover why you made the mistake, but also how you felt leading up to it and after. You will also learn if you need to reassess your goals. Maybe you are doing too much too soon. You can uncover this if you made multiple similar smaller mistakes before this one.

The biggest question I think is, "What benefit did I believe this action would bring me?" One of the major lessons I had to learn on my journey was those fleeting moments of happiness or satisfaction were not worth the negative effects that followed, and I made mistakes based off this small moment in time.

The best way to overcome that is to stay present and in the moment. A great book I recommend reading is *The Power of Now* by Eckhart Tolle. The majority of our mistakes are not made in the present moment. We make mistakes because we either dwell on something in the past or lust after something in the future we believe will make us happy.

HAPPINESS IS NOW. YOU HAVE EVERYTHING YOU NEED TO FEEL COMPLETE AND PERFECT RIGHT NOW.

Remember: Aim for progress, not perfection. Even if you make the same mistake one hundred times, it's okay as long as you learn something from it every time. Most of the time we never take a moment to first admit that we did something we didn't want to, yet find out why it happened. By incorporating this practice we can learn to make successes out of our mistakes.

Use this section of the book if you want to make a mistake or you crave something unhealthy.

Sleep

Sleep is a very underrated category that a lot of people don't think about when it comes to losing weight but trust me, it is vitally important. How we feel during the day greatly depends on the amount and quality of sleep we got the night before. Eating a healthy diet, getting your butt outside to exercise each day, and doing your best in your daily life requires more than just motivation. You need to feel good and have the energy from sufficient rest to power through your day. Quality sleep is essential.

One thing you may not know about me is I have always had trouble sleeping. I have somewhat of a restless mind. Over the course of the last few years I have practiced many things to get my sleep cycle in check and I am going to teach you just how to do that today.

We need to have somewhat of a plan when it comes to a restful nights sleep that you can rely on consistently. One of the most important things to do is to learn to avoid caffeine, salt, sugar, alcohol which is going to make it so much harder to get to sleep and stay asleep long enough to wake up feeling refreshed. One thing a lot of people don't realize is sleeping is the time that our body takes to repair. It is the longest period we go without food so essentially when we are sleeping, we are fasting. Fasting is when the body is at full rest and is not digesting food. If you didn't know this, eating food actually takes up more energy than anything you could ever possibly do. Thats how hard your body has to work to assimilate nutrients and energy into a usable form. A big thing that I recommend is having your last meal 3-4 hours before bed so that your body can use the time to restore instead of digest. Also not having any liquids an hour before bedtime will keep you from waking up in the middle of the night having to use the restroom.

Our sleep cycles are meant to be in sync with the sun. We rise when the sun comes up, and we sleep and rest when the sun goes down. If you think about the time before there was electricity, we wouldn't have had any other choice but to do this. We would not be out gathering food or being active in the middle of the night because we wouldn't be able to see anything or assess if there were any dangers around us. This is how we will get back in sync with our body's natural sleep-wake cycle, your circadian rhythm is one of the most important techniques for achieving good sleep.

Set your "bedtime" around when the sun goes down. No staying up till 1am watching Netflix! Get into bed at the same time every single night and be free from distractions. You typically want to pick a time around not only when the sun goes down but when you generally get tired. If you typically go to bed around midnight and wake up at 6, try pushing your bedtime earlier and earlier each day for a week until you get to a more normal time. We want to be getting 8 hours of rest each night. When I say "rest" that doesn't always mean sleeping. If your sleep schedule is messed up, the best thing you can do, is set a bed time, and get into bed and just lay there in the dark and rest.

If you keep a regular sleep schedule, going to bed and getting up at the same time each day, you will feel more refreshed and energized than if you sleep the same number of hours at different times. Consistency is very important.

If you're getting enough sleep every night, you should wake up naturally without an alarm. If you need an alarm clock to wake up on time, you may need to set an earlier bedtime. If you have to be to work every day at 7 am and you would normally wake up at 5 am to start getting ready, you may need to lay down at 8:30 pm every night to ensure you fall asleep by 9 pm if you need eight hours of sleep. I go to bed every single night at 9 pm and I wake up every single day at 6. I don't even have a reason to wake up this early its what my body just naturally does everyday.

The light from a television or computer suppresses your melatonin production and stimulates your mind instead of relaxing it, creating unnecessary stress.

You also want your bedroom to be as dark as possible, the temperature as comfortable as possible, the cooler the better and minimize any noise you possibly can. Turn off the television and computer. The light from a television or computer suppresses your melatonin production and stimulates your mind instead of relaxing it, creating unnecessary stress. If you need something to fall asleep to, listen to an inspiring audiobook, read or practice relaxation exercises. Instead of reading from your phone or kindle or flipping through tumblr for hours before bed, read an actual paperback book.

One thing I like to do as I lay in bed while trying to fall asleep is to think of all the wonderful things that happened during the day and pick which one was the best. Thinking of positive things before bed is a wonderful way to improve your life. As we think of good things before sleep, we go to bed feeling good and that is what our subconscious mind resonates with for the eight to nine hours we are unconscious.

Natural Beauty Tips

Beauty is something I am questioned about a lot, and I'm also passionate about my minimalistic and all-natural beauty routine. The biggest beauty tip I can give you is not what you put on your skin, but what you put into your body. Since you've already got that part down by living the LEAN & CLEAN lifestyle, let's go over why it's also important to watch what you use on the outside of your body.

Did you know the average person uses, at the very least, ten different products on their body every single day? The scary part is these ten products can have an average of over 130 chemicals in them, chemicals our body has to excrete because our skin, even though it is a barrier, acts like a sponge and absorbs everything we put onto it.

USE ALL-NATURAL PRODUCTS

The best thing you can do is to use natural products you recognize. Instead of using lotion or makeup remover, you can use coconut oil. Instead of using perfume, use essential oils such as lavender, orange, or eucalyptus.

The idea here is to simplify your beauty routine. You do not need twelve different face creams to fight off wrinkles and premature aging. Marketing has led us to believe we need all these products, but it isn't true. As we all know and have experienced, these products never work as they do in the television or magazine ads. It is much more important to eat a healthy whole foods diet, stay hydrated, stay away from caffeine, and get enough rest every night.

Making your own soap or shampoo is tedious and time-consuming so for convenience sake, learn what to look for when you are buying products.

RECOGNIZE THE INGREDIENTS

Look for ingredients you know, like shea butter, jojoba oil, lemon essence, etc. If you do not know what an ingredient is, look it up on your phone while you are in the store. Sometimes ingredients may sound weird, like zinc oxide, but are okay. Here is a list of ingredients you want to avoid.

1,4-dioxane: A known animal carcinogen and probable human carcinogen.

Aluminum Chlorohydrate: An astringent used as a topical antiperspirant or topical body deodorant. Aluminum is a neurotoxin that alters the function of the blood-brain barrier, linking it to Alzheimer's disease and cancer.

Ammonia: A compound used in hair dyes and bleaches. It releases a caustic, pungent gas that irritates the eyes and respiratory tract.

Dibutyl phthalate: A chemical plasticizer found in nail polish and mascara to prevent cracking. Can cause birth defects, and harms male reproductive organs.

Formaldehyde: A preservative and disinfectant classified by the EPA as a probable human carcinogen. Found in mascara and eye shadows, formaldehyde can cause nausea, coughing, and asthma symptoms, as well as burning sensations in the eyes, nose, and throat.

Lead Actetate: Prevalent in hair dyes. A known developmental and neurotoxin. Hydroquinone: Found in lotions and facial products. Hydroquinone is a skin-bleaching chemical, a possible carcinogen, neurotoxin, and skin sensitizer.

Mercury: Used in mascara and other cosmetics as a preservative and antibacterial agent listed as "thimerosal." Mercury can damage brain function in humans even at very low levels.

Methylparaben, Ethylparaben, Butylparaben and Isoparapben: The most common preservatives used in cosmetics to prevent bacterial and fungal growth. Parabens mimic the hormone estrogen, which can play the role in developing certain cancers such as breast cancer.

NO ANIMAL TESTING

Animal testing isn't what a lot of people think. Rats and bunnies are not slathered with lotion and they bounce around smelling good. They are directly tested with high concentrations of chemicals to see what type of reaction is produced. These animals never get to see the light of day, play in the grass, or have any natural experiences in their lives. I have directly witnessed the inside of an animal testing lab when I worked a previous job. I was shocked they didn't use bunnies or rats, but they used dogs. I had to walk through this lab, and I was horrified when I heard them all barking and crying. These animals are put in cages in dark rooms where they have little space. The most they are capable of doing is turning around in a circle, and they do this over and over and over again because they are distraught and terrified from being trapped.

There is no reason for animal testing, especially when it comes to something as superficial as beauty products. If a company is using animals to test their products, one thing you can know for certain is those products are filled with chemicals and are not safe. Please do not support animal testing. Below is a link for the PETA website where you can see which companies are currently using animals to test their products. **http://features.peta.org/cruelty-free-company-search/index.aspx**

Most eco-friendly companies use ethical practices regarding animal testing, chemicals, and recyclables, or compostable packaging. I like to find companies I can trust and stick with them because I know their standards are safe and ethical. It makes my life a whole lot easier when I keep the products I use to a minimum and stick with the companies I know and trust. Some of my favorites I have come to use over the years are:

Dr. Bronners: I use their soaps for every cleaning job in the house from dishes to cleaning the floors, as well as my skin and bathing my pets.

Pacifica Beauty: One of my favorite all-natural beauty brands. My favorite products are their supernova mascara and their nail polishes.

100% Pure: This company makes their products from fruit pigments and is my go-to for face powder, eyeshadow, and haircare.

DENTAL HYGIENE

Oral hygiene is simple once you get some good products and a good routine down. Let's start with toothpaste.

You might not think much about the ingredients in your toothpaste compared to the ingredients in your food or even other personal care products because you're not using much of it and you spit it out anyways, right? Our mouths are one of the most absorbent places on our bodies, which is why lots of medications are administered orally. Over the course of our lifetime we will use close to twenty gallons of toothpaste. That's a lot of toothpaste! Even if you spit most of it out, some of the chemicals in it make their way into your bloodstream.

This is why you need to be careful when choosing toothpaste. Many popular brands contain harmful ingredients that can hurt our bodies. Making the switch to an all-natural toothpaste is a simple and painless change.

Some of these common harmful ingredients are sodium lauryl sulfate (SLS), artificial sweeteners, triclosan, fluoride, propylene glycol, and diethanolamine (DEA).

These ingredients have side effects ranging from irritants and allergies to hormone imbalances and neurological or endocrine disruption.

There are some great all-natural toothpastes on the market like Desert Essence and Earth Paste, which can be a little more expensive than the toxic conventional brands. However, if you're on tight budget, you can make your own toothpaste at home.

Brushing your teeth twice a day is the key to keeping your mouth healthy and happy, but one of the most important habits to include in your tooth care regime is flossing.

Unlike a toothbrush, which cleans the tops and outer surfaces of the teeth and gums, floss is an interdental cleaner. It's designed specifically to clean the tight spaces between the teeth and the gap between the base of the teeth and the gums. These are places a toothbrush can't reach. While antimicrobial mouthwash can kill the bacteria that form plaque, it can't remove the stubborn tartar and bits of food lodged in these places.

Another handy ingredient is clove oil. If you ever have sore gums, bleeding, a toothache, or pretty much any discomfort in your mouth, use a few drops of clove oil on the end of a cotton swab and lightly swab the area. It works wonders!

HOMEMADE
Peppermint Toothpaste

Ingredients:
1 tsp. baking soda
1 drop peppermint or clove oil
A few drops of water

Method:
Mix in a bowl until the paste is formed. Place some on your toothbrush, and brush your teeth.

Acne

Not only is eating the LEAN & CLEAN lifestyle great for losing weight, but it is fantastic for your skin as well. I have never personally struggled with severe or cystic acne, but my husband, Derek, has experienced the benefits of a low-fat starch-based diet for acne. We also have read a number of personal testimonials where people have effortlessly healed their acne through eating whole plant foods. I know this is a huge thing people struggle with in their lives, and Derek's experience shows how you can heal even painful cystic acne.

A little bit of a background, Derek started getting painful cystic acne when he was around fifteen years old. Since that time he has tried every conceivable method in order to bring relief to his skin, including using dangerous pharmaceuticals such as Accutane. Now at twenty-nine years old, he can finally say his skin is the clearest it has ever been, and he doesn't have any issues keeping it that way.

No one is exactly sure what causes acne. There are a number of different theories, but nothing is entirely conclusive. Some people believe the main reasons are overt fat consumption, especially oils and animal products, hormones, insulin is one of them, and compromised digestion. We believe it's a combination of all three.

Eating a whole food plant-based diet is a huge step in the right direction, and many people have been able to clear their skin by making this change. It wasn't easy for Derek, and the next step he took which showed great improvement in his skin was taking a strong probiotic. Derek has never had good digestion. Even when you eat an ideal diet, if your digestion is bad, those foods can sit in your stomach and create a whirlwind of bacteria that is usually excreted through your skin. People with acne are more likely to experience symptoms of gastrointestinal distress like constipation and heartburn.

There is a strong correlation between the health of your gut and your skin health. Taking a probiotic introduces billions of probiotics, which help build your gut flora, and improves your digestion. We've recommended either the 25 billion or 50 billion probiotic. Both work great and the 50 billion is just double the potency. Here is the 25 billion vegan probiotic by NOW that you can find here: **https://highcarb.co/ probiotic**

> People with acne are more likely to experience symptoms of gastrointestinal distress like constipation and heartburn.
>
> There is a strong correlation between the health of your gut and your skin health.

We both believe acne is an internal issue, which means eating the right foods and healing from within, but we also believe there are a few things you can do externally to help your skin.

Derek uses an oil-free acne wash by Alba organics called "Acne Dote" to clean his skin and remove excess oil. Afterward he uses a mixture of 1/3 vegetable glycerin, 1/3 water, 1/3 witch hazel to moisturize. It's important if you have acne not to introduce more oil to your skin, either through your diet or the products you use.

It is important to experiment with supplementation. There is one mineral which is a common deficiency among acne sufferers. That mineral is zinc. Zinc promotes healthy skin by carrying vitamin A to our skin and promotes apoptosis, which is the process with which the skin renews itself. Zinc also reduces inflammation in the body. While there are many different forms of zinc you can use to supplement, the best kind is zinc picolinate. You should take 25-50mg per day, and you must take zinc with food to avoid nausea.

We believe if you focus on these four lifestyle shifts: eating LEAN & CLEAN, taking a daily probiotic, experimenting with zinc supplements, and using an oil-free products on your skin, your acne will clear up with dramatic results. It may take some time to clear up, but you will notice fantastic results if you stick with it.

Exercise Plan

Following the meal plan in LEAN & CLEAN will provide great results and account for the majority of your weight loss. This book isn't just about weight loss, though. Yes, exercise will help you shed pounds, look leaner and more toned, but the main benefit is well-being. Exercising thirty minutes per day releases endorphins, which are those feel-good chemicals you experience after a workout. This is helpful when starting a healthy lifestyle because these chemicals make you feel vibrant! The better you feel, the more confidence you have, and this increases your chances of remaining on a healthy lifestyle ten-fold.

Now before you start thinking "OMG, I have to work out every day?" It's not backbreaking work every day. I think you will find my recommendations easy, fun, and simple to include in your current day-to-day life.

When it comes to building and increasing our fitness, it is much simpler than what you may think. While there are many ways you can go about exercising your body such as HIIT, hiring a personal trainer or going to group classes at a local gym, I don't recommend them for most people. They are often expensive, too difficult for your fitness level, or far too hard on your body.

The LEAN & CLEAN lifestyle is about having a healthy relationship with food and we want to extend that relationship to exercise as well. We want to focus on gentle exercises which will be easy on our bodies. If we start with exercises that are too difficult for us right now, we can end up injuring ourselves. The two activities I recommend for weight loss and building fitness levels are brisk walking and cycling. Both of these exercises are both gentle on the body and can be done by almost anyone. You can also use low impact exercise equipment as well, like an elliptical trainer.

For five days of the week, focus on doing light movement. This can be walking your dog, going for a bike ride to the store or taking a yoga class. Pick two other days that work for you, and we will work on increasing your fitness level on those two days.

Many people exercise a lot, but they never push their body. They focus on increasing their distance instead of increasing the intensity of the workout. If you consistently push your body twice a week, you will improve your fitness level while accelerating your results.

This type of training is essential to getting leaner and fitter. Most people think the more exercise you do, the better. This type of thinking is backward. Almost anyone can go out and run or walk a half-marathon. I did it when I was at my heaviest weight, and it took me forever, but I did it.

The point is to focus on increasing your speed rather than distance. Once you've run your first 5k run, most people focus on longer distances rather than improving their 5k time.

The fastest people who run any distance will

be much leaner than those who are much slower. People who are overweight can finish a marathon, but it would be rare for an overweight person to finish 26.2 miles in less than four hours.

THIS IS THE KEY TO THE LEAN & CLEAN FITNESS PLAN.

I suggest setting aside one hour to do a fitness session. One hour gives you time to do a proper warm-up, give your maximum effort, and cool down. These are all important parts of a session. It's important to include all three parts to reduce the risk of injury and stay consistent over the long-term. Spend about two hours per week building your fitness. Maybe you can do more, but that is a good place to start.

The three components I mentioned above are the warm-up, max effort and cool down. Let's discuss what each one means and its purpose.

THE THREE COMPONENTS OF A WORKOUT

A WARM-UP is the time you spend walking or cycling at an easy pace. The pace needs to be brisk, but light enough so you're able to talk, your breathing is light, and it's comfortable for you to walk. During this time your heart rate will typically be around 105- 129 beats per minute. This is also known as the fat-burning or recovery zone. Not only is it important for fat burning to exercise in this zone, but it warms your muscles for the max effort you will do next.

THE MAX EFFORT is when you push your body to a level which isn't comfortable for you. Don't worry, this is for a short period of time. You will experience muscle fatigue and heavy breathing. During this time, you want your heart rate to stay between 155-180 beats per minute. This zone will build your fitness level.

THE COOL DOWN is the time when you will recover from the max effort. You will walk or cycle at a comfortable pace. Heart rate again needs to stay between 105-129 beats per minute. The purpose of the cool down is to let your body recover and give time for your heart rate to lower itself back to its normal beat. If you pushed yourself, the cool down will become a time where you experience a rush of feel-good endorphins from working so hard in the max effort.

THE 1-HOUR *Workout*

Let's put it all together based on a one-hour workout interval.
WARM-UP: 30-35 minutes
MAX EFFORT: 3-10 minutes
COOL DOWN: 20-25 minutes

The easiest way to perform at a maximum effort is by either cycling up a hill or walking up steps or a hill. When we move our bodies vertically, it is stressful and raises our heart rate to a level where we are not comfortable. With this in mind, think about where you will be able to do this. If there aren't any hills, you can still do a max effort while cycling on flat land. It's more difficult to walk at max effort so push yourself to turn that time into a jog or run.

For example, if it takes you about one minute to ride up a hill you are using for your max effort, you can do laps on that hill. Ride to the top, ride down, ride up, ride down, ride up, ride down. That way, you still have at least three minutes of max effort. This is similar to interval training.

If you have access to a gym, you can ride the stationary bike, use the elliptical trainer, walk on a treadmill or hit up the stair stepper. There

are many different options for getting a great cardio workout. Find which one works best for you and your location.

Now, if you are novice with regards to fitness and overweight, you may want to skip the max effort altogether and focus on keeping a brisk pace while walking or cycling. As you lose weight, it will become easier to push your body. If you choose to do max efforts, spend only five to fifteen minutes per week in that zone.

What would a typical week look like while following the LEAN & CLEAN lifestyle?

Daily movement is important. It isn't always practical with our busy lives so do the best you can. Here's an example.

Typical Week ON LEAN & CLEAN

MONDAY | 5000 steps
30 minutes of brisk walking with my pets

TUESDAY | 4000 STEPS
25 minutes of brisk walking during my lunch break

WEDNESDAY | 10,000 STEPS
1-hour workout using the treadmill, max effort for 6 min.

THURSDAY | OFF DAY
Prior commitments and not able to get in my daily movement

FRIDAY | 5000 STEPS
30 minutes of brisk walking with my pets

SATURDAY | 10,000 STEPS
1-hour brisk walk with hiking group, max effort for 5 min.

SUNDAY | BIKE
30-minute bike ride to and from grocery store

Be creative with how you can get in daily movement. It can take a number of different forms. You can take your pets for a long walk, ride your bike to the grocery store, or spend thirty minutes on the treadmill in your local gym.

You can walk, ride, or run, for people who are more physically fit, to and from school or work a number of times per week. Using your body as a form of transportation is a slick way to get in your daily movement.

You can get a stationary bike trainer so you can ride your road bicycle indoors. 'Zwift' is a great app you can use indoors with your bike trainer.

The important thing is consistency and to be easy on yourself. Even if you only have fifteen minutes, go out for a quick walk. Maintain a habit of daily movement.

TRACKING YOUR PROGRESS

When focusing on improving your fitness during your max-effort workouts, knowing your current heart rate is important. Far too often people exercise too hard when they need to work at an easier pace. Instead of a heart rate between 105-129 BPM, which stands for Beats Per Minute, it could be in the 140's or 150's.

Keeping your heart rate in the proper zone is important so your workouts are more effective. Your heart rate needs to be low about 90-95% of the time for optimal fat burning and so you aren't working out too hard.

There are many different options to measure your heart rate. Amazon has a great selection of heart rate monitors. We've always used devices with a heart rate strap, but there are plenty of options you wear like a watch which don't require a chest strap. There are even chest straps that will pair up with your smart phone as well. The prices for these different options span a large range, but many are within the $40-$60 range. We've found it well worth the investment.

Another great way to track your progress is to use the Strava application (www.strava.com). You can pair GPS fitness devices with the website and track your activities. You can compare yourself to others based on different segments. It is an awesome and interactive app that is free to use. You can also get the Strava app for your smart phone and track your walks, rides, and runs that way, too.

If building your fitness is important to you, then tracking it is imperative. If you want to be able to improve something in your life, measuring it to see your progress is crucial.

MY STEP COUNTER

If building your fitness isn't that important to you, then invest in an activity monitor. I use a Garmin vivofit and what I love about it is that I can easily track how many steps I've walked each day. Since I work at home, getting in daily movement requires a bit more effort.

What I like to do is a set goals for myself each day for how many steps I want to walk. It could be 5,000, 10,000 or even 15,000 steps in one day. This goal gives me something to work towards and instead of driving to the store around the block, I'll just walk and get my steps in for the day. It's a simple way to get my daily movement in and I highly recommend it.

MAKE MOVEMENT SOCIAL

Building your fitness by yourself can be a bit boring at times. Why not find a friend or family member to exercise with, or join a local cycling/hiking/walking club. Check Facebook and Meetup.com for local groups. If you make exercise a social event, it will become much more fun and exercising with other people who will hold you accountable as well. If you exercise with people who are fitter than you, it will push you to the next level. If you prefer to exercise by yourself due to logistics or personal preference, listen to positive audiobooks while on your walks or bike riding.

FINAL TIPS

Make sure you are hydrated. Drink one half to a full quart (liter) of water before your exercise session and bring a small bottle with you to your session. Do not eat within one hour of starting your workout so your food has time to digest.

If you have been sedentary most of your life and haven't participated in much sport, you want to take things easy when you first start. The majority of people we encounter don't have a strong fitness background so our recommendations are for people just getting started so they can progress without injury. If you are capable of doing HIIT programs like the Bikini Body Guide, that is fine. Those kinds of workouts may be too difficult for someone who is new to daily movement in their life.

Remember: The majority of your results will come from your food choices. Incorporating exercise and fitness in to your life is a part of a healthy lifestyle. Keep it simple, fun, and comfortable!

Tracking Your Progress

Measuring and weighing yourself is an important part of any weight-loss regime because... Well, this is the reason we are here, right? One thing I want to outline is how often you should weigh yourself, why you should trust measurements over weight, and how to do all of this properly without going insane.

Using the scale to track your progress every day is not a good indicator because there are a multitude of factors that figure into how much you weigh on a day-to-day basis. You can gain muscle and lose fat, but gain weight. Your weight fluctuates from differences in atmospheric pressure, how much water weight you are holding that day due to the temperature outside or how much salt you had the day before, along with what time you weigh yourself, and how much food and water is in your belly. Let's be honest. Would you care what the number on the scale said if you got to your dream dress size? No, you wouldn't. If you look and feel fabulous, that's all that matters. There is a time and a place for weighing yourself and it can be useful in tracking your progress even if it is just to brag to your friends or to show your doctor how well you are doing on your new plant-based diet.

Would you care what the number on the scale said if you got to your dream dress size? No, you wouldn't. If you look and feel fabulous, that's all that matters.

I always recommend people weigh themselves at the beginning and once a month after that. The best time to weigh yourself is first thing in the morning after you've gone to the bathroom and before you've ingested anything. Make sure you are naked and you place the scale on the same floor to weigh yourself every time. That is all you need to do to get the most accurate measurement.

Now I know you are thinking, "Seriously Hannah? You want me to weigh myself once a month? How will I even know if this is working?" Well my friend, you will know from taking your body measurements. It is a much more useful tool than taking your weight because if you lose an inch of fat on your belly, you will see it on the tape measure whereas on the scale it isn't a concrete analysis.

BELOW ARE THE AREAS YOU WANT TO MEASURE EVERY WEEK.

BUST: Place the measuring tape across your nipples and measure around the largest part of your chest. Exhale before taking your measurement. Be sure to keep the tape parallel to the floor. Don't forget to write down the measurements.

CHEST: Place the measuring tape just under your breasts/pecs and measure around the torso. Exhale again while keeping the tape parallel to the floor. Don't forget to write down the measurements.

WAIST: Place the measuring tape about a half inch above your belly button, the narrowest part of your waist, to measure around your torso. When measuring your waist, exhale and measure before inhaling again. Don't forget to write down the measurements.

HIPS: Place the measuring tape across the widest part of your hips/buttocks and measure all the way around while keeping the tape parallel to the floor. Take your measurement and write it down.

ARMS: Place the measuring tape around the widest part of your bicep, usually about two inches down from your shoulder. Take your measurement and write it down.

THIGHS: Place the measuring tape around the largest park of your upper leg, usually about two inches down from the top of your thigh. Take your measurement and write it down.

Write these numbers down in a small book and keep it in a safe place. This will give you a great idea of how your body changes every week as well as giving you the feedback you need to make any changes to get to your goals. To keep your measurements more consistent, look for markers on your body to use as a guide. A marker is something like a freckle, mole, birthmark, or tattoo that is always there and never moves. As long as it is close to where the largest part of your arm, thigh, or waist, you will get the correct measurement every time.

Setting Realistic Goals

You have to lose ten pounds before you can lose thirty pounds. No, I'm not being a smart-ass here. This is a fact. One thing people do that becomes frustrating is they set their goals too high at first. They say, "I want to lose forty pounds by summer." That's a great goal to have, but it can become daunting. Especially when you step on the scale every week to find you only lost one or two pounds. That's another reason why you should only weigh yourself once a month. If your goals are too high at first, it will feel like it will take forever and you will never get there.

We need to set realistic goals. Saying "I'm never going to eat junk food again" or "I will work out for two hours every single day" is silly. Let's be honest. Most of the time we set up no-win situations for ourselves by our unrealistic expectations about how "flawless" we can be and how much weight we can lose in X number of days. These statements may look innocent, but if they form the foundation of the way we approach our goals, we are in for serious disappointment.

We may say, "I'll only eat a foolproof diet until I get to my goal weight," but this is a lie and we know it. Saying this to ourselves is detrimental because the moment we slip up

"I want to eat twenty Lean & Clean meals this week and let myself have one meal 'off' so I can go out with my husband for a date." That's a great goal!

and have something we're not supposed to, guess what happens? We binge.

Many times binging leads to a cycle of trying to be perfect and then screwing up over and over again, which is a big reason we can never reach our goals.

You are human. You will want to eat something you're not supposed to, have a beer with friends, or lay on the couch all day without moving. That doesn't mean you messed up nor are you a failure, so don't expect every day to be perfect.

Setting realistic goals means we want to think of where we want to be in a month and set small goals on how we plan to get there. These goals don't have to focus your weight, either. Some of the most successful people who have done the LEAN & CLEAN lifestyle never even weighed themselves.

Psychologist Dr. Doug Lisle says the best goals to set are to eat clean and get outside. You could say, "I want to eat twenty LEAN & CLEAN meals this week and let myself have one meal "off" so I can go out with my husband for a date." That's a great goal!

Another goal is to get outside and be active for thirty minutes a day, even if it is only walking around the block.

I know the reason you are here is weight loss, but you need to look at your habits and meet yourself where you are now. If you don't regularly exercise, an awesome goal is to walk 5,000 steps every day.

If you eat "convenience foods" frequently for lunch, which are full of additives, salt, and chemicals, a great goal to set is to pack a lunch every day for work.

The best way to be successful at losing weight is to focus on losing ten pounds at a time. That's why I opened this chapter with, "You need to lose ten pounds before you can lose thirty pounds." If you weigh 168 pounds right now, think about how awesome it will be when you get to the 150's. Once you get to the 150's, you can work your way down to the 140's and the 130's etc.

I know at the beginning of my weight-loss journey I said to myself, "Man, I need to lose seventy-some pounds!" It was daunting. I didn't take it one step at a time, which set me up for serious failure. I tried to be perfect, but it only led me to screwing up and binging.

Once I said, "Okay, I'm going to take this ten pounds at a time," everything got a lot easier. I accomplished something big when I went from 150 pounds to 140 pounds because it became my goal, and I made it! It motivated me to keep going. My past approach of thinking, "Oh, I made it to 140 pounds, but I still have twenty-five pounds to lose," sounded more like I had failed because I wasn't yet at my goal.

You can also set fitness goals, like running a 5k in a certain amount of time. You can set measurement goals. If you have a 30-inch waist, set a goal to get a 29-inch reading and go from there.

Be proud of yourself when you reach these mini goals because this is how we achieve those huge life feats!

You can do this. One day at a time!

Maintenance Versus
WEIGHT LOSS

A lot of people ask me, "Hannah, do I have to eat this way forever?" The answer is yes and no. Maintaining your weight is much different than losing weight. You do not need to be as strict. I've found that when I was most successful with my weight loss was when I followed this program to a T.

Since I have reached my optimal weight it has been easy to maintain it by following a whole foods plant-based diet. So yes, you need to follow a whole foods plant-based diet as much as possible to easily maintain your weight and health for life.

That does not mean you can't go out to eat with your friends or have something with oil, salt, or sugar ever again. I eat vegan junk food every now and then. It happens, and I do not eat 100% perfect all the time. Derek and I also go out to eat once or twice a week. While I no longer crave foods with oil, salt, and refined sugar, sometimes I have a vegan burger and fries at a restaurant or I'll sample all the delicious vegan food at an event like VegFest.

You don't need to be perfect when you are in maintenance mode. As long as you make sure the majority, around 90%, of your diet is whole plant-based foods, you will be fine. People even find they can add in salt and refined sugar in small amounts without any trouble maintaining their weight.

The LEAN & CLEAN lifestyle is not about deprivation or isolating yourself from social occasions. But when you are in weight-loss mode, it is best to stick to the program because you will get there much faster, easier, and without losing your mind.

The most common message I get from people usually goes something like this.

"Hey Hannah, my name is Jenny. I have been following the Starch Solution by the book for three months and I have not lost a single pound. I am 5'6 and weigh 140 pounds, and I want to get down between 115-120 pounds.

I work out four times a week for an hour at the gym, doing cardio and strength training, plus fifteen minutes of yoga each morning.

HERE IS WHAT I EAT IN A DAY.
BREAKFAST: Oatmeal with a tbsp of coconut sugar, 1 apple, and a dash of cinnamon. Snack: 3 pieces of bread with store-bought hummus.
LUNCH: A sushi bowl with 3 cups white rice, veggies, 1/2 avocado, and soy sauce.
DINNER: A vegan pizza with tons of veggies. No Daiya cheese, just sauce.
DESSERT: Banana nice cream: 3 bananas, cocoa powder, PB2 powdered peanut butter.

What am I doing wrong? Why am I not losing weight? Am I eating too much? Do I need less fat? Please help me!"

Here is the issue. These people are eating what I call a perfect maintenance diet. The only real issue here is the food they is too stimulating and calorically dense, which makes them eat more than they naturally would. Another thing you can see is there are not many vegetables in her diet except for a little in a sushi bowl and on top of pizza. Vegetables are the biggest weight loss secret ever, and you need to fill up on them as much as possible.

This is not an unhealthy diet nor will you eat an unhealthy amount of food. It is a healthy way of eating, and you will be in good health if you eat like Jenny every day, but it probably is not enough to get her to her goals. Her body weight is in the normal range for her height and weight. She doesn't want to become unnaturally thin, but she wants to look fantastic and feel fit.

I'm giving you this example because the majority of people who contact me are in this situation. They are at a normal weight, but want to look their best. This is a common thing. A lot of us want this, and it is easy to achieve by following this program.

I was in the same position as Jenny. I was stuck at the weight of 138 pounds, give or take a few pounds, for nearly a year. It was easy for me to lose the first fifty pounds and go from an obese BMI down to a normal BMI, but I simply wanted to look my best. Following everything in this guide were the things that helped me get down to my natural weight.

In order to lose the last twenty-five pounds, I had to be strict with my diet. It wasn't hard because I was still able to eat as much as I wanted, but I couldn't have a few vegan chips and go out to eat once a week, or have a beer with my friends and become successful because it stimulated my appetite too much and kept me from my goals.

Once I applied the LEAN & CLEAN principles, I could not believe how easy and quick it was for me to get down to my ideal weight. It took me three months, and once I got there I was able to be more lenient with my diet.

If you want to achieve your goals as fast and as painlessly as possible, stick to the LEAN & CLEAN lifestyle as much as you can. Trust me, it's worth it. Once you get to your goals, you can have your vegan cake and eat it, too. Well, every once in a while.

How Much Should I Eat?

Eat as much as you need to feel full and satisfied. Now you know how the body works and we cannot overpower our hunger drive. The most important key to a healthy and sustainable diet is satiation. As long as you eat whole plant foods and do not overstimulate your taste buds with salt, sugar, and oil, you will do just fine. The key to losing weight is not starvation. The key to weight loss is eating nutrition dense foods with fewer calories that give you the nutrients and energy your body needs. This means you can and should eat until you are full and happy!

This guide is meant to be just that—a guide. You will find three different recipes for each day so you will have options, along with portion amounts for what an average person who is losing weight should eat.

Remember: All of us are different, and we all live different lives. You may need to eat more than what is in this guide, or you may not want to eat as much. That's fine. Do what works for your body and your life.

If you are not full, and you want to accelerate your weight loss, have a salad before each meal and eat more vegetables like broccoli, cauliflower, zucchini, or celery to fill you up before you eat your starches.

> Remember: All of us are different, and we all live different lives. You may need to eat more than what is in this guide, or you may not want to eat as much. That's fine. Do what works for your body and your life.

Remember: When we are overweight our body dials down our hunger drive so we can safely lose weight. One thing I know is you will not be as hungry on this plan than if we gave you a bunch of processed vegan snacks to eat. You will naturally eat the perfect amount of food, as nature designed us to, when you eat food in its whole food plant- based form.

If there are recipes you don't like, don't eat them. I do not expect you to like all the recipes in this book. Eat the meals you enjoy and find satisfying. Most people eat the same foods every week, day in and day out.

Whether they eat a standard diet or a whole food plant-based diet, they eat the same thing 90% of the time. They have cereal for breakfast, a sandwich for lunch, and rotate four to five different dinners, but they do not cycle through 100 different recipes.

We do this because it's in our nature to find easy, satisfying meals and repeat those over and over again. We do this because we know we will enjoy our meal. This guide is not complicated, and it will give you a lot of ideas for preparing easy meals so you can find a new weekly rotation of meals to eat. Make the ones you like and throw out the ones you don't like or you think are too complicated for you to make now. Within time, and once you feel better about your body, you'll want to try all the recipes.

If you find yourself craving junk food, like chocolate, chips, or ice cream, know this is generally never true hunger. A craving occurs either because you are hungry or you emotionally crave the experience those foods give you.

If you find yourself in this situation ask yourself, "Do I want to eat a plate of brown rice and vegetables or do I only want a chocolate bar?" If you answer you want chocolate, that's a craving. You can either make something healthy from one of the recipes in this book to satisfy your craving, like chocolate banana ice cream in the snack section, or you can realize you truly aren't hungry and let it pass. These moments are crucial in your weight-loss journey because they can turn into snap decisions at a friend's house or restaurant. Once you decide to eat junk food, it will make you feel bad about yourself ten minutes later.

Remember: You always have a choice and the power to make a good decision. You will be much happier with yourself if you make a healthy alternative or realize you aren't hungry and eat later when you are actually hungry. Always confirm you have some type of healthy food with you when you leave the house, no matter what, and eat regular meals so you have enough energy and nutrition to keep yourself satisfied.

The Social Difficulties
OF BEING PLANT-BASED

You know what's interesting? The most difficult part of eating a plant-based diet is the social aspect of it. Whether you're a cooked vegan or raw vegan or somewhere in between, the people around you sometimes find it so weird you no longer eat animal products, they will ask you about your eating habits.

"So wait. You don't eat meat or drink milk? Surely you must eat cheese, yes? No cheese? Surely you must eat fish, everyone eats fish. No fish? But how do you get your protein?"

The above is the type of conversation you could have when you explain to someone that you no longer eat any animal products. People will become curious about you because it seems so far out of their reality that you don't eat meat, dairy, eggs, fish, or fowl anymore. After they inquire about every little bit of your food intake, they will typically follow up with something like this.

"Well I don't eat THAT much meat, a little bit. But cheese, I love cheese. I could never give it up." - Typical meat-eating person

If you've eaten a plant-based diet for some time, you'll chuckle at this because this is almost always how these conversations go. It begins with someone asking you many questions only to follow up with a justification for how they live their life.

I don't think people who eat animal products are bad people at all, but isn't it funny how many people who eat animal products justify their eating habits in one way or another to you? It's almost as if they know on some level that what they are doing isn't necessarily the best for them and it causes harm to other beings.

The majority of people who eat animal products do so out of ignorance. No, they aren't being rude. They aren't educated about the science and facts surrounding animal products and how detrimental it is to their health, the environment, and the animals.

Ignorance of the ramifications of their food choices is only one reason why they continue to eat animal products. They eat that way because it is an ingrained habit, something almost all of us grew up doing. There are few people in the world who grew up plant-based. Those are the few lucky ones.

With this understanding, when people challenge you about eating a plant-based diet with jokes or rude remarks, you must realize this is not a reflection of you or how you live. It is a reflection of them and how they feel about themselves and their life. There is nothing wrong with that so we should never condemn or make others feel inferior about this.

Understand that when you tell someone you eat a plant-based diet or a vegan diet, it's a statement in and of itself. That statement rings loud and clear in their ears, and it becomes confrontational at times. One of the main reasons I believe people make rude comments

Plant-Based Social Life ➤

about eating a plant-based diet is because those who do not want you to conform to their reality. They want you to change back to eating animal products and unhealthy foods because if you resume your prior eating habits, it will make them feel better about their poor choices.

If you're new to eating plant-based, you may have family members or friends that egg you on to eat a little bit of their food. Sorry for the pun. They may say, "Oh, come on, have a hamburger. One hamburger won't hurt you!" This is pretty typical so expect it. Stand your ground, though. Don't let social pressure affect the choice you've made for the health of your body, the animals, and the planet.

It is sometimes difficult to say no in those circumstances. But as you do it more often, the easier it becomes. It is also important to plan ahead. If you're on your way to a family gathering or to a friend's place to eat, it is best to assume they don't know what you can and cannot eat. This means supplying your own food in these circumstances is the best thing to do. While this may feel a little weird at first, it will take a lot of stress off the host and hostess because he or she may not have any idea of what to make for you. While many may not eat a plant-based diet, they are educated on the topic enough to know what you can and cannot eat.

Make a double-sized portion of one of your favorite recipes from the recipe section so you can share it with others and show them how tasty simple plant foods are. I almost guarantee they will be shocked when they learn there are not any animal products in it, they will feel

better after eating it, and they will most likely ask you for the recipe.

Eating out at restaurants is another situation which is often difficult for new vegans. Always choose vegan restaurants or restaurants that advertise vegan options.

A great website to find these places is **www. happycow.net**. If you're going to a restaurant where you are unsure of the options available to you, eat a meal at home before you leave for the restaurant. As weird as this sounds, it will save you from making poor choices. If you've already eaten, it gives you more options from which to choose. Instead of ordering an entrée, you can order a side salad and feel satisfied because you've eaten beforehand.

When ordering from a menu that you are unsure of, let the waiter or waitress know you are allergic to meat, dairy, eggs, fish, and fowl. They will relay that information back to the chef who prepares your food. The last thing they want is to have an ambulance at their doorstep because a customer had an allergic reaction. If you say "I don't eat animal products," they will not understand you and may cook your meal with butter, milk, or fish oil. Most restaurants are getting better at offering more plant-based options as veganism becomes more popular.

If you don't have any plant-based or vegan friends, then make it a priority to meet these people in your area. It is so refreshing to speak with people who share this important lifestyle with you. It's great because fellow vegans and plant-based eaters understand you. You have something in common, and for most people

> *Make a double-sized portion of one of your favorite recipes from the recipe section so you can share it with others and show them how tasty simple plant foods are. I almost guarantee they will be shocked…*

Lean & Clean | highcarbhannah.co **89**

veganism is an important part of their life.

With the growing network of people on Facebook, Youtube, Instagram and other social media platforms, it has become easier to meet and make friends. Search for local vegan groups on Facebook or check out **www.meetup.com** for groups in your area. It will make things much more enjoyable for you to meet more like-minded friends who follow the same lifestyle.

Another important topic I think should be discussed is about our significant others. A common story is someone meets a great person, and they both eat a Standard American Diet. When one of them starts eating a plant-based diet, that person wants their partner to eat plant-based diet along with them.

This can be a tricky situation because you started a relationship together, but you changed and now you want them to change to match how your life now. This isn't fair to the other party involved because this has become a condition of the relationship. You may think if your partner were plant-based, you'd be happier or love them more. It is not good to think like this, especially if you want your partner to change.

You must love your significant other, no matter what, with unconditional love. If they sense you have conditions for your love for them based on their eating habits, it can cause resentment in the relationship. By showing your partner unconditional love, they feel better about themselves and from there you can educate them on the benefits of plant-based eating.

Make sure they know you love them no matter what they eat. This will create the space they may need to make the transition. Live by being an example of health, positivity, and love so those around you will become intrigued and follow your daring lead.

For those of you who are single and want to meet a vegan partner, put out that wish to the universe. Write out the type of partner you desire in the form of a script. List the qualities and traits you love and think of all the emotions you would feel if you found that person.

People do change. If your partner is unsupportive, and you have grown apart, you may feel like you need to end your relationship. Sometimes relationships end. But do not let one lifestyle change turn into the be-all end-all of a relationship. Most people are supportive when they see someone make positive life changes. Giving your partner space, preparing healthy meals, and letting them sample your food, will allow him or her the opportunity to make the decision on their own.

Lean & Clean Guide

TO EATING OUT

highly recommend that you do not eat out for the fourteen days of this reset plan. It is hard to find oil-free, salt-free, unrefined sugar-free food at a restaurant. However, you may find you need to eat out during the reset, so below is a list of the best options to choose. Not all of them may be salt-free or sugar-free, but they are some of the healthiest options offered.

This guide is for you to reference when you are done with the 14-day reset and want to go out with friends. Your food will have salt in it, and that's okay. One meal a week isn't going to throw you off course from your goals. Yes, you can still go out to eat with your friends!

Remember: Avoid oil first. Avoid excess salt next and sugar after that. Say you go out to eat and they make a pad Thai without oil, but it still has salt and sugar in it. That's okay. I ask for an extra side of the noodles and split the main entrée with a friend, which cuts the salt in half, or I ask for the sauce on the side. Sometimes you can get salt-free roasted potatoes, but they have oil in them. Order something without oil instead, like rice or a baked potato.

Sugar is the least of our worries, but keep in mind restaurants want their food to taste delectable so they add lots of oil, salt, and sugar to their foods to make it intoxicating. If you can cut out one or two of these culprits, you will be fine.

Restaurant Recommendations

THAI/ASIAN RESTAURANTS

I like fresh spring rolls made with rice paper, not fried. Most Thai places I go to will make any stir-fry dish without oil if you ask. You can order steamed rice and veggies, and ask if they have oil-free sauces.

They also offer a variety of vegan soups that are usually oil-free or can be made without oil, like miso soup, ramen, etc. A lot of Asian restaurants also serve sushi so you can have cucumber rolls, with or without avocado, or any veggie roll, and skip the soy sauce.

MEXICAN RESTAURANTS

Whenever I go out for Mexican food, I always get rice, beans — not refried because they are always made with lard *yuck*, corn, pico de gallo, guacamole, and a side of corn tortillas. These places are often a bit hard because those free chips and salsa are tempting, but a trick is to order your corn tortillas first so when they bring out the chips you can eat the salsa and guacamole with your oil-free tortillas. Yum!

Spanish rice is also a good option because it's usually made without oil, but check to be sure.

Most flour tortillas will have oil in them, but another option is to get a taco salad with all the beans, corn, tomatoes, avocado and veggies you like without the fried tortilla toppings or the fried tortilla-shell bowl.

INDIAN RESTAURANTS

A lot of the dishes are vegan the way they are prepared, but the main thing to ask is if they use ghee, which is clarified butter or oil in their dishes. Poppadom/Papadum, Chapatti, Puri/Poori and Rotti are all vegan, but take an extra precaution and double-check with your server. I love eating vegetable curry, veggie vindaloo, Chana masala/Chole, chickpea curry, sambar. Always order an extra side of rice and a side of steamed vegetables. Most places will prepare your dish without salt or low in salt so don't be afraid to ask.

ORGANIC/VEGAN CAFES

Eating healthy has become popular so there are many organic and vegan cafes where you can easily find a smoothie, salad, sandwich, or acai bowl to keep you going. A great website for finding local vegan restaurants is **www. happycow.net**

AMERICAN

Steakhouses, burger joints, or the local family restaurants are tough, but usually you can get a baked potato, a side salad with balsamic vinegar, a fruit bowl, oatmeal, or vegan soup.

FAST FOOD

Sometimes we find ourselves in a pickle and we need to eat so here are some of the best options at the most popular fast food restaurants.
WENDY'S: Baked potato. Ask for no sour cream or eat with ketchup or hot sauce.

SUBWAY: Six-inch sub, white bread, with all the veggies and sweet onion terryaki dressing or mustard.
CHIPOTLE: Burrito bowl with salsa, lettuce, corn, lime juice.
DOMINOS: Thin crust with marinara and all the veggies you like.
DENNY'S: Build your own burger with Amy's vegan patty and all the veggies.
NOODLES & COMPANY: Order the Indonesian peanut sautée. It's so good!
PANERA BREAD: Black bean soup with ciabatta bread to dip in it.
STARBUCKS: Oatmeal, classic or blueberry flavors.
TACO BELL: Order the black bean burrito al fresco style (without cheese and sour cream.)
WHITE CASTLE: Veggie sliders are vegan, but not healthy. However, that's your best option if it's the only place you have available.

HOW TO ORDER YOUR SIDE DISHES
- Ask for steamed, no oil, low salt after verifying everything is vegan.
- Ask for an extra side of rice and either a side salad without dressing or a side of steamed veggies to go with my meal.

BEST SIDE DISHES
- Baked potato
- Fruit bowls with nuts, seeds, coconut
- Side salad with lemon wedges or balsamic dressing
- Steamed rice
- Steamed vegetables

ENTREES

When ordering entrees, choose baked or steamed or ask your server if the dish can be prepared by baking or steaming it.

LEAN & CLEAN
Food Pyramid

Eat Your Vegetables!

Seriously. I know your mom told you this all the time as a kid, but eating a lot of vegetables is important to the LEAN & CLEAN lifestyle.

Why? Vegetables are the most nutrient dense, high-fiber foods you can eat. I'm not talking about potatoes here. I'm talking about non-starchy vegetables, like broccoli, spinach, asparagus, carrots, mushrooms. Even vegetables that are considered fruits, like tomatoes, bell peppers, and cucumbers are also part of this list.

Vegetables and greens are critical for weight loss, but also the most health-benefiting foods to eat. You can get all of your iron in a few cups of spinach, all your calcium from broccoli, your vitamin A from carrots, and the list goes on and on. The best thing about vegetables, especially if you are serious about weight loss, is they fill you up with few calories.

You may have noticed from the LEAN & CLEAN food pyramid that vegetables and greens were on the bottom. That's because you can eat as many as you possibly want. I'll say that again. You can eat as much as you want and it is important to eat as many as you can.

A lot of people message me and say, "Hannah, I've been eating super clean for the last three months, no oil, no sugar, little salt, and I cannot lose weight." When I ask them what they are eating, 99% admit their diet is void of vegetables and greens. I think a lot of people focus on eating whole starches, fruits, beans, and lentils while forgetting about this one important food group.

Optimal nourishment is a huge reason vegetables are important on a daily basis. You need to eat your vegetables because you need a supply of vitamins every day. Some vitamins can be stored for future use and others cannot. When we run low on nutrients our bodies crave more food and we usually reach for junk food.

Some of the vitamins that can be stored in the body are fat-soluble vitamins such as vitamins A, D, and E, but for the body to run optimally we also need water-soluble vitamins. Found within this group are all of the B-complex vitamins, including vitamins B1, B2, B3, B5, B6, B12, biotin, choline, folic acid, and vitamin C.

We need these water-soluble vitamins every single day because they can't be stored in the body. We need to replenish them to stay healthy. The only vitamin we cannot get is vitamin B12 and I recommend taking Complement. It has vitamin B12, D3 and Omega-3s. Learn more about the brand I take and recommend: **https://highcarb.co/complement**

If you ever had issues with constipation or not going regularly, you won't after you eat your veggies. Poor digestion leads to a lot of problems. In fact, the health of our gut is vitally important to the health of our entire body. Poor digestion can lead to diseases of the colon, stomach, and bladder. It can cause rapid aging and unnecessary weight gain as you read about in the chapter entitled *The Importance of Good Digestion*.

Dietary fiber is critical for the health of our digestive tract. Not only on a daily basis, but also on a meal-by-meal and snack-by-snack basis. Food cannot move through our digestive tract in a healthy way unless it is fiber-rich, and vegetables are some of the richest sources of fiber in existence.

Your vegetables don't have to be boring. If you need a little salt or sriracha to eat them, then add it in for more flavor. My favorite mix of vegetables is bell pepper, onion, mushroom, and spinach sautéed in water with added garlic powder, onion powder, and a little nutritional yeast. I also love eating steamed broccoli and cauliflower with a little of the butternut squash hummus or steamed asparagus with nutritional yeast and lemon juice. Sometimes I add a little hot sauce or salt-free salsa for kick to these recipes, but I can honestly say I eat at least one to two pounds of vegetables a day and you should, too.

You also do not have to eat them plain on their own like this. Add in steamed potatoes or rice for the perfect meal. Most of the recipes throughout the meal plan are packed with veggies. I sneak them in whenever possible. Feel free to add more vegetables or swap out what you don't like for others you prefer.

Remember: You can always eat a huge plate of veggies as a snack or even for breakfast.

How To Shop For Less

I am a firm believer that a healthy diet is inexpensive and easy to maintain once you get going. In the beginning, you will buy ingredients you're not used to buying like nutritional yeast or other items you have never consumed in large quantities. "I need how much brown rice?" Adjusting your shopping with a few of the following tips will save you a lot of money.

BUYING IN BULK

Bulk buying can save you a substantial amount of money over time. Most people don't know this, but most grocery stores are willing to sell case quantities of food at a discount. Bulk items that are great to buy on this meal plan are potatoes, brown rice, and cases of bananas. We always buy 20-40lb bags of rice. Not only does it save us lots of trips to the grocery store, but also lots of money and wasted packaging. If you purchase a case of bananas, wait until they are nice and spotty and freeze them for a few months' worth of smoothies or nice cream stock.

BUYING ORGANIC

I always recommend and promote eating organic whenever possible. If you either cannot afford it or the conventional foods are more available to you, then purchase conventional produce. There is a list of foods you should always buy as organic referred to as *The Dirty Dozen* because those foods have the highest

levels of pesticide residues on them if they are not labeled organic.

These twelve foods are exposed to environmental toxins so try to buy these foods organic, even if you buy everything else conventional.

THE 12 MOST Contaminated Foods

- Corn
- Apples
- Bell Peppers
- Celery
- Nectarines/ Peaches
- Strawberries
- Cherries
- Pears
- Grapes
- Lettuce/Greens
- Potatoes
- Spinach

I want to point out that sugar could be listed as the thirteenth item because pesticides are used in sugar cane fields.

If these items are pricey in the organic section of your grocery store, look for frozen. Frozen is usually cheaper and contains more nutrients because they are frozen right after they are picked, and they are usually picked at the peak of ripeness. Some foods that are not necessary to buy organic are bananas, avocados, pineapple, mangoes, and broccoli. It's up to you whether you can afford to buy organic. If you can't, don't worry about it. You are doing your body such a good deed by feeding it whole plant foods. In the long run you will save yourself so much time

and frustration by not paying for medicine and medical bills because of your good health.

GREAT PLACES TO SHOP

FARMERS MARKETS: Farmers markets are one of the best and cheapest places to get produce. You typically get the highest quality food when you shop here because you are buying locally grown food. Many times you will buy the food within hours of when it was picked. Most of these farmers are able to sell it to you cheap because you are cutting out the middleman.

Derek and I can get an entire week's worth of food at our local farmers market for a fraction of what we'd spend at the grocery store. One time we found 25-pound bags of potatoes for $10 dollars! To find your local farmers market, search in Google to find the location and the time it runs. Bring your reusable bags because you will find some incredible deals!

Another tip is to go on the last day of the market near closing time. This is when farmers will bargain with you because there won't be another market for a week and they want to get rid of everything. Prices are often cut in half or even less, and you can negotiate with them to get some incredible deals on stuff.

FOOD CO-OP: Food cooperatives are another cheap place to get local-sourced foods. Produce is often the cheap at these places while a lot of other packaged items is expensive. This is where local farmers go to get rid of the extra produce they didn't sell at the markets. So if you miss your local farmers market, this should be your next stop.

BULK STORES: Sam's Club, Costco, and other bulk stores are great places to buy large quantities of food, but you need a membership to do so. These places are best for families, in my opinion, because you can buy a large quantity of food every week and get your money's worth in comparison to what you paid for your membership.

THRIVE MARKET: Thrive Market is one of my favorite places to shop because I'm lazy, and I love buying stuff online. There is a small membership fee, but they also offer free delivery. They carry things you usually have to run around to get like tahini, red lentils, or nutritional yeast. If you don't have a lot of stores close to you, this is a great option.

TRADER JOE'S: Trader Joe's is another store offering low prices because most of their produce is locally sourced. They will also allow you to buy bananas and other items in bulk cases if you ask, and will even give you a discount. They have a great in-house brand which is inexpensive.

Summary

A lot of information was presented to you in the last section of the book. Allow me to reiterate and summarize some of the valuable information to help you understand it better. The main message that you need to understand is simple.

EAT WHOLE PLANT FOODS.

Whole plant foods include starches, vegetables, fruits, legumes, nuts, and seeds. We need to eat these foods until we are satisfied because that is the only way to be successful. When I say successful, I do not mean that solely in terms of weight loss, but also in overall health. Weight loss will come when the overall health of our body has improved, and this happens over time.

When we come from a past of dieting, eating a poor fiber-less diet which is deficient in nutrients and water, our bodies will not run optimally. Our hormones don't function correctly, which can lead to a multitude of problems like depression, insomnia, weight gain, lethargy, and the list goes on and on. Eating a whole food plant-based diet corrects this over time.

You don't need to worry about calories when you eat a whole food, plant-based diet. Your appetite will regulate itself as your body becomes healthier and your hormones normalize. Our bodies are smart. Each body knows how much it should weigh to be healthy and it knows how much you need to eat to reach your optimal weight. In order for your body to be able to communicate that to you, you have to eat the right foods.

Sugar, flour, oil, salt, and other processed foods are what disrupts your body's ability to regulate the hormone ghrelin, which is how your body communicates to you how hungry you are and how much you need to eat.

We need the nutrients, fiber, and water in whole plant foods to bulk up our diet and give us the volume of foods to trigger our satiety mechanism. Our natural hunger responses will only work when we eat these foods because it's the only way we can get the proper caloric density within this volume to regulate our natural hunger signals. You do not need to deliberately eat a caloric deficit because your body will automatically do that when you eat this way.

When we have excess fat on our body, those fat cells release the hormone leptin, which dials down our hunger drive until we reach our body's natural weight. This means if you eat a whole food, plant-based diet, you will naturally eat a caloric deficit. Our appetite changes depending on how much activity and mental demands we have day to day, but over time your appetite mechanism will drive you to have a caloric deficit that will get you to your natural weight.

Eat plenty of vegetables, starches, fruits, legumes, with a few nuts and seeds in the 14-day meal plan and let your body take care of the rest. **It's that simple. Now let's get to the fun part. Eating.**

THE 14-DAY
Meal Plan

Shopping Guide Tips

The items listed are those you will need each week. For best results, make sure you have them on hand. You will not need to buy new items each week. For example, you may have a jar of maple syrup or many of the spices already in your pantry.

MAKING A LIST

Check off every week what you already have, and make a list of the items you will need. You can buy frozen vegetables or fruits instead of fresh. Buy either dry or canned beans, whichever you prefer.

WORK WITH YOUR BUDGET

Take a quick glance through the recipes each week so you will get an idea of what you will cook and what types of vegetables, sauces, and spices you will want with the dishes. Do what is convenient for you and your budget. For example: Instead of buying four different types of vegetables to go along with your starches, buy a frozen vegetable medley.

DO NOT BUY WHAT YOU DO NOT LIKE.

You can always substitute something else. It is not necessary to have the exact spices on hand if you are an experienced cook. You can always omit spices you don't like in favor of something you prefer.

BUY IN BULK TO SAVE $$

To save money, buy your rice, potatoes, and oats in bulk so you will not need to buy them again in week two. When you make your grocery list each week, double-check that you have these items or add them to the list for the week.

DECIDE WHICH ADD-ONS YOU WANT

This shopping guide only covers the base meals without any add-ons because those are optional.

READ THE LABELS

When buying canned or packaged goods, look for products without salt, sugars, or oils. A lot of times you can find things without salt, but it will contain a little added sugar. Go for that option if an alternative is not available. You can also buy dry beans and cook them yourself if you have the time.

Snacks & Desserts

} If you are hungry in between meals you can always have snacks or desserts that are oil-free and high carb. Here are some ideas for you.

A FEW PIECES OF FRUIT:

Have 1-2 pieces of your favorite fruit in between meals such as banana, mango, apples, a bowl of pineapple or a bowl of mixed fruit.

VEGGIES WITH FAT FREE HUMMUS:

Have a bowl of mixed veggies such as carrots, celery, cucumber, broccoli or whatever you like. You can find a store bought hummus or blend together 1 can of chickpeas, 2 cloves garlic, 2 tbsp lemon juice, 1 tsp salt. You can also use this hummus on your salads.

BANANA NICE CREAM:

Banana nice cream makes a great sweet treat and you can change the flavor very easily. Blend together 2-3 frozen bananas, 2-3 tbsp water along with 1-2 tbsp flavoring powder you like: cacao, acai, cinnamon, powdered peanut butter.

CORN TORTILLAS BAKED WITH SALSA:

A very easy go to snack if you want something crunchy and salty. Take 2-3 corn tortillas, slice into triangles and sprinkle with the juice of half a lime, a pinch of salt, cumin, chili powder or whatever seasonings you like. Bake in the oven on 400°F (204°C) for about 15 min or until crispy. Serve with salsa, hummus, or another oil free sauce.

FAT-FREE AIR POPPED POPCORN:

Have a few cups of oil-free/fat-free popcorn.

BROWN RICE CAKES WITH SPREAD:

Spread a few brown rice cakes with jam or hummus.

SPROUTED GRAIN BREAD WITH SPREAD:

Have 1-2 pieces sprouted grain bread (ezekiel is a great brand) with a low fat spread like jam, hummus, or salsa.

Snacks are great to have but if you feel like any of these wont satisfy you then it's probably time for an actual meal. Snacks should serve as small portions to get you through to the next meal so they shouldn't be large in size but with that in mind you should also never go hungry.

If you find that you are hungrier than expected and your meals aren't filling you up, make your meals a little larger by multiplying the amount of starches in the dish by 25% or 50%. For example, if a meal says to eat 2 baked potatoes then have 3 potatoes. If a meal says to have 2 cups of rice, then have 2 1/2 or 3 cups.

Also make sure you are drinking enough water as stated in the *Bloating & Constipation* chapter. Sometimes we are just dehydrated and I know from my own experience I will feel hungry but then have a 12 ounce glass of water and a few minutes later I won't be hungry at all. This isn't saying replace food with water, if you have some water and still feel hungry then you need to eat so have a snack or a meal.

Important Notes

COOKING RICE

I didn't include rice cooking instructions along with each of the recipes because it would've become redundant. When I say, "2 cups steamed rice" in the recipes, that is about 1/2 to 2/3 cups of dry rice. 1 cup of dry rice will yield between 3-4 cups of cooked rice.

I highly recommend purchasing a rice cooker if you don't already have one. They are inexpensive and smaller ones are about $20. If you have an Instant Pot (or any other pressure cooker brand) they do a great job of cooking rice as well. What's so great about rice cookers is that you can put the water and rice in the cooker pot, hit the on button and then in 20-30 minutes, you'll have perfectly cooked rice. They are a game changer.

They also have a keep warm function so that when the rice is finished, it will stay warm for as long as you need. Say you cook rice in the morning and have extra, just leave it in there. Then when you get home from work or school, just plug the rice cooker back in and leave it on the "keep warm" function and it will reheat your rice.

Some rice cookers also have a steaming tray which can be convenient for steaming vegetables. Also keep in mind that certain cookers have a minimum amount of rice needed so they operate properly. If a rice cooker says it needs 2 cups as a minimum, it means 2 rice cups, which equates to 1-1/2 standard US cup sizes.

This might start to get a little confusing now but bear with me. When you buy a rice cooker, it comes with a small measuring cup. One of those measuring cups is the equivalent size of 3/4 cups (180mL).

When buying a rice cooker, buy the size that fits your needs. If you are just cooking rice for yourself, a small rice cooker is all you'll need. If you're cooking rice for yourself and family, you'll want a larger one. Again, keep in mind the minimum amount of rice needed for it to operate properly.

MEAL PREP ASTERISKS

In many of the recipes through the meal plan, you will see an asterisks (*) next to an item. It might be Pre-made Salsa* or Sweet Potatoes*. The asterisk means that the instructions and ingredients for that item are in the Meal Prep chapters. As you'll learn, preparation is an important part of succeeding on the LEAN & CLEAN lifestyle.

SHREDDED HASHBROWNS

In the meal plan, there are a few recipes that call for shredded hashbrowns. I made note on one of them that I get these bags of shredded hashbrowns from Trader Joes. If you do not have access to this particular store, search in the frozen section for bags of shredded hashbrowns that do not contain any oil or seasonings. Your store may or may not have them.

If your only option are packaged hashbrowns that have loads of oil or seasonings in them, you can always make your own. Just use 1 or 2 medium potatoes and shred them using a food processor.

We prefer the bagged hashbrowns because of their convenience but do the best you can with what you have.

Week One

Week One Shopping Guide

STARCHES

1 1-pound bag of oats
1 2-pound bag brown or white rice
1 5-pound bag white potatoes
3 large sweet potatoes
1 15oz can black beans
2 15oz cans garbanzo beans
1 15oz can kidney beans
1 1-pound bag red lentils
1 1-pound bag quinoa
1 12-ounce box gluten-free (GF) pasta

VEGETABLES

1 1-pound box mixed greens
1 10-ounce bag frozen corn
1 10-ounce bag spinach, fresh or frozen
2 medium white onions or 1 red onion
2 medium zucchini
4 Roma tomatoes, also called plum tomatoes
3 tomatoes
2 15oz-cans chopped tomatoes
3 6oz cans tomato paste
3 stalks of celery
1 20-ounce bag frozen shredded hash browns
1 10-ounce bag frozen mixed veggies
1 red pepper
3 small mushrooms
3 medium cucumbers
2 carrots
1 avocado
1 bunch scallions
1 bunch cilantro
1 garlic bulb
~ Add any other favorite veggies
1 package of roasted nori (no oil)

FRUITS

1 16-ounce bag frozen mixed berries
1 16-ounce bag frozen strawberries
1 lemon
2 limes
10 bananas
3 large mangoes or 1 16-ounce bags frozen mango
1 cup mulberries (or raisins, or dried berries)
2 pounds Medjool dates

SWEETNERS, SPICES, NUTS & SEEDS

Cinnamon
Cumin
Chili powder
Onion powder
Garlic powder
Dried dill
Curry powder
Italian seasoning
Paprika
1 jar tahini or almond butter
1/4 cup raw cashews
Mustard
Hot sauce
Nutritional yeast
Buckwheat groats
Coconut flakes

QUICK CONVERSIONS

1 pound = 454g
15oz = 443mL
6oz = 178mL
16 ounces = 1 pound

Week One Meal Prep

Meal prep is instrumental for making your life a whole lot easier, especially if you have a job to go to every day and a family to cook for every night. This section will keep you sane during those busy times. If you do not want to do any meal prep and you have the time to cook all your meals fresh, feel free to skip this section.

> **THIS WEEK'S MEAL PREP** includes preparing a few things in advance for breakfasts, lunches, and salads, so when you need to make the sweet potato salad on Day 4 you can throw it in a bowl and whisk your dressing together before heading out the door for work.

BANANAS

It is always crucial to have at least 12 frozen bananas in your freezer at the beginning of the week. These are great for smoothies, banana milk, and nice cream. The best way to do this is always buy 12 extra bananas each week. Let them sit out until they get nice and spotty. Peel them and freeze them in either a large plastic container or a big freezer bag.

QUINOA

Mix 2 cups of dry quinoa with 5 cups of water in a medium saucepan and bring to a boil on your stove. Cover and reduce heat to simmer. Cook for 20 minutes. Refrigerate for up to one week in an airtight container.

BAKED SWEET POTATOES

Pre-cooking sweet potatoes for the week ahead is a huge time-saver. They are an amazing snack and taste incredible cold. We will pre-cook our entire bag for the week ahead. Preheat your oven to 450°F (232°C). Place your potatoes on a baking sheet. Do not poke holes or make any cuts in them. Bake for about 35-45 minutes or until they are soft all the way through when pierced with a fork. Refrigerate for up to one week in an airtight container.

GRANOLA FOR BREAKFASTS AND SNACKS

1   cup of oats
1   cup of mulberries (sub raisins or dried berries if you cannot find mulberries)
8   Medjool dates, pitted.
1/4 cup of water
1   tsp cinnamon

Combine all ingredients in a food processor and process until well combined. Spread out on parchment paper and place on a baking tray, bake at 350°F (176°C) for 20-25 minutes. Place in a big storage bag or tightly sealed container. Feel free to double this recipe. I always double it because it's so good!

KETCHUP

1/2 cup water
1 6-ounce can tomato paste
4 Medjool dates, soaked in water for 1 hour
1 tbsp apple cider vinegar
1/4 tsp garlic powder
1/4 tsp dried oregano

If your dates are hard, soak them for 1 hour in the 1/2 cup of water then blend all the ingredients on high until smooth. Soft dates do not need to be soaked. Refrigerate for up to one week in an airtight container. **LOW-SALT OPTION:** Add 1/4 tsp salt before mixing.

TZATZIKI SAUCE

1/4 cup raw cashews, soaked for one hour
2 tbsp lemon juice
1 large or 2 small garlic cloves
1/2 cup cucumber, peeled & chopped
1 tsp dried dill
1/3 cup water

This sauce is used for the falafel, Mediterranean salad, and is used as a dip for veggies. Take all your ingredients and blend on high in a blender. Refrigerate for up to 1 week in an airtight container. **LOW-SALT OPTION:** Add 1/4 tsp salt before mixing.

SWEET MUSTARD DRESSING

4 tbsp tahini or almond butter
6 dates, soaked in water for 1 hour
2 tbsp salt free mustard or 1 tsp mustard powder
1 tsp garlic powder
3/4 cup water

If your dates are hard, soak them for 1 hour in the 3/4 cup of water then blend all the ingredients on high until smooth. Soft dates do not need to be soaked. Refrigerate for up to one week in an airtight container. **LOW-SALT OPTION:** Add 1/4 tsp salt before mixing.

PRE-MADE SALSA

4 Roma tomatoes
1/4 of a medium red onion
1/4 cup fresh cilantro
~ Juice of one lime

Chop your tomatoes, red onion, and cilantro into bite-sized pieces. Drizzle with lime juice. Refrigerate in an airtight container for up to one week.

THAT'S IT FOR FOOD PREP THIS WEEK. Spending an hour or two in the kitchen at the beginning of each week is worth the time you save while cooking these things, especially if you are starving or running out the door.

Day 1

BREAKFAST: Berry Oatmeal

BASE
1	cup oats
2	cups water
1/2	cup frozen or fresh berries
~	Sprinkle of cinnamon

ADD-ONS
1-2	chopped Medjool dates
2	tbsp buckwheat groats

METHOD
Combine oats and water in a small saucepan and bring to a boil. Reduce heat to low and let cook 5 minutes or until all the water is absorbed. Stir occasionally. Place oats in bowl and sprinkle with cinnamon. Top with berries and other toppings.

LUNCH: Taco Salad

BASE
1	cup greens
1/2	cup black beans
1/2	cup corn
1	cup steamed brown rice (1/3 cup dry)
~	Pre-made salsa*
1/4	small avocado
1/2	lime, juice of

METHOD
Cook rice as per the instructions on the package. You only need 1 cup of cooked rice. Place greens in half of a bowl and rice in the other half. Add beans and corn. Top with salsa and avocado. Drizzle with lime juice.

Day 1

DINNER: Pizza Fries

BASE
3   medium potatoes, peeled and cut lengthwise into strips
1   tsp each: onion powder, garlic powder, paprika
~   Pre-made ketchup*

ADD-ONS
~   Nutritional yeast

METHOD
Preheat oven to 425°F (218°C). Place fries in a large bowl and toss with spices. Arrange fries on a pan prepared with parchment paper or on a baking rack. Bake for 30 minutes or until cooked through. Remove from oven. Dip in pre-made ketchup. Top the fries with nutritional yeast and fresh chopped basil for extra flavor.

Day 2

BREAKFAST: *Green Smoothie Bowl*

BASE

2   frozen bananas
1   chopped fresh banana
1   fresh mango diced or
1   cup frozen mango
1   cup water
1   cup spinach

ADD-ONS

1   tbsp pre-made granola*
1   tbsp coconut flakes

METHOD

Blend frozen bananas, spinach, water and half the mango. Pour into a bowl and top with chopped banana, and the rest of the mango and optional toppings.

LUNCH: *Quinoa Sweet Potato Mash*

BASE

1   cup quinoa cooked*
1   large sweet potato pre-cooked*
1/2   tsp garlic powder
1/2   tsp cumin
2   tbsp sweet mustard dressing*

ADD-ONS

~   Any veggies you like or
      on a bed of greens
1/2   cup beans

METHOD

Place your potato and quinoa (cooked in meal prep) in a large bowl. Add the seasonings and mash them together. Add any additional toppings or veggies you like. Drizzle with dressing and serve.

Day 2

DINNER: Chili

BASE

1	can kidney beans (rinsed well)
1	cup dry red lentils
1	can (15oz or 443mL) chopped tomatoes
1	can (6oz or 178mL) tomato paste
1/2	onion, chopped
2	tbsp chili powder
1	tbsp each of cumin and garlic powder
3	stalks celery, chopped
4	cups water, may need more at the end

METHOD

Throw everything in a saucepan, bring to a boil, reduce heat and let it simmer for 40 minutes or cook for 17 minutes in a pressure cooker. This recipe makes a few servings so you can eat it over salad, rice, or potatoes for other meals this week. Enjoy 2 cups of chili served over 1-2 cups steamed brown rice for dinner. Save the remainder of the chili for dinner tomorrow.

TIP: Chili is a great meal to make whenever you have leftover veggies, beans, or rice. For the chili I made for the photo, I added leftover quinoa and pinto beans that were in the refrigerator so don't be afraid to be creative with the recipes and use what you have. Not only will you use up leftovers that might have gone bad, but it also makes you a better cook because you familiarize yourself with tastes and flavors that work well together.

Day 3

BREAKFAST: *Hash Brown Bake*

BASE
1 pound frozen shredded hash browns
1 tsp each, garlic, onion, paprika powder
1/4 cup each, chopped: red pepper,
  onion, spinach, mushrooms OR
1 cup frozen vegetable mix

METHOD
Toss your hash browns in seasonings. Add your vegetables and mix well. Set oven to 450°F (232°C). Place mixture in a 9-inch baking dish (I use a pie pan) or spread out the mixture flat onto a non stick cookie sheet and bake until crispy, about 20 minutes. Serve with pre-made ketchup.

TIP: Trader Joe's has great oil-free, sodium-free frozen hash browns. If you can't find sodium free hash browns, omit the seasonings when preparing.

LUNCH: *Mediterranean Salad*

BASE
1 cups greens
3/4 cup garbanzo beans
3/4 cup cooked quinoa*
1/2 tomato, chopped
1/2 cucumber, chopped
2 tbsp tzatziki dressing*

ADD-ONS
~ Diced onion or chives
~ Sun dried tomatoes

METHOD
Rinse the beans. Put the greens, beans and quinoa (cooked in meal prep) in a bowl. Chop cucumber and tomato into bite-sized pieces and toss. Top with tzatziki dressing and serve.

Day 3

DINNER: Loaded Baked Potato

BASE
2 large baked potatoes
1-2 cups chili (leftovers)

ADD-ONS
~ Nutritional yeast
~ Chopped scallions

METHOD
Poke a few holes in the potatoes, wrap with tin foil and cook in oven on 425°F (218°C) until soft, about 45 min. Once cooked, cut in half and top with chili and other toppings.

Day 4

BREAKFAST: *Mango Oatmeal*

BASE
1   cup oats
1   mango, pitted and diced or
1   cup frozen mango
2   cups water

ADD-ONS
1-2   chopped Medjool dates
1   tbsp buckwheat groats

METHOD
Combine oats and water in a small saucepan and bring to a boil. Reduce heat to low and let cook 5 minutes or until all the water is absorbed. Stir occasionally. Place oats in bowl and add the mango. Add additional toppings if you wish.

TIP: Trader Joe's carries the best frozen mango. If you can't get fresh mango, this is the next best thing.

LUNCH: *Salad with Sweet Potato*

BASE
2   large sweet potatoes*
2   cups greens

ADD-ONS
1   tomato, chopped
1/2   cucumber, chopped
2   tbsp tzatziki dressing or
     sweet mustard*

METHOD
Take your pre-cooked sweet potato out of the fridge. Chop it into bite-sized pieces and serve potato over the salad. Chop any additional veggies you like to add to the salad. Drizzle with dressing and enjoy!

Day 4

DINNER: Cheesy Mashed Potatoes

BASE

3	medium potatoes
2	medium zucchini
1/4	cup nutritional yeast
1	tsp garlic powder
1/4	lemon, juice of
~	scallions
~	black pepper

METHOD

Peel your potatoes and zucchini. Chop both into 2-inch chunks and boil them until soft, about 15 minutes. Drain all except 1/4 cup of the cooking water. Add nutritional yeast to vegetables and remaining water and mash until you get a smooth consistency. Add lemon juice, scallions, black pepper, and a little more nutritional yeast to the top.

Day 5

BREAKFAST: Strawberry Smoothie Bowl

BASE
2	cups frozen strawberries
2	frozen bananas
1	fresh banana, chopped
3	cups water

ADD-ONS
2	tbsp pumpkin seeds
~	Other fruit

METHOD
Add water, frozen bananas, and strawberries into blender and blend until smooth. Add the chopped fresh banana and top with pumpkin seeds and coconut flakes if you like. Eat with a spoon and chew your smoothie.

LUNCH: Rice & Beans

BASE
1	cup steamed brown rice (1/3 cup dry)
1	cup black beans
1	tsp each cumin, chili powder
~	Pre-made salsa*

ADD-ONS
1-2	cups greens
~	Chopped bell pepper

METHOD
Rinse your black beans well until there are no more bubbles. The bubbles are what make you gassy! Mix your cooked rice, beans and spices together and top with salsa.

TIP: A great way to use up leftover ingredients is to add it to your lunches or salads. I add leftover stews and thick soups to the top of my rice bowls or add them cold to salads to give them more flavor. Add any leftover chili made earlier this week or any leftover avocado halves you may have to this.

Day 5

DINNER: Vegetable Sushi Rolls

BASE
4   sheets nori
2   cups steamed white or brown rice
1   carrot
1/2 cucumber
1/2 avocado

METHOD
Cook the white rice and allow it to cool before using. Julienne your carrot and cucumber so the result is long thin slices. Spread 1/4 of your rice over a nori sheet, add carrot, cucumber, and avocado to the middle. Roll all of it together, pressing so the ingredients are tight within the roll. Repeat this process until all the rice is gone.

Day 6

BREAKFAST: *Granola Fruit Cereal*

BASE
1   cup pre-made granola*
1   fresh banana, chopped
1   frozen banana
1   cup frozen strawberries
1   cup water
1   tsp cinnamon

METHOD
Combine your frozen banana, water, strawberries, and cinnamon in your blender. Blend until smooth. Chop your fresh banana and add to your granola. Pour your banana milk over top. Add any additional fruits or toppings.

LUNCH: *Quinoa Salad*

BASE
1   cup cooked quinoa (1/3 cup dry)
2   cups greens
1   carrot shredded
1/2   cup edamame or garbanzo beans

ADD-ONS
1/4   cup dry cranberries or
       2 chopped dates
3   tbsp sweet mustard dressing*
~   Other veggies you like, such as
       tomato, beets, sprouts, etc.

METHOD
Cook quinoa according to package. Chop up veggies and place all ingredients in a large bowl. Drizzle with dressing and serve.

Day 6

DINNER: Falafels & Salad

BASE

1	cup garbanzo beans
1/4	cup oats
1	Medjool date
1/2	tsp each garlic powder, cumin, paprika
1/4	cup chopped onion
1	tbsp lemon juice
2	tbsp fresh cilantro

SALAD

3	cups greens
1	tomato, chopped
1/2	cucumber, chopped
2	tbsp tzatziki dressing*

METHOD

Preheat oven to 375°F (190°C). Process all the falafel ingredients in your food processor until a dough forms. Take 1/4 of the mixture and roll into a ball and then press into a patty. Repeat until you have 4 falafels. Place on a nonstick pan and put in the oven on the middle rack for 20 minutes. Flip them over and cook another 15 minutes. Arrange your salad and chop up your tomato and cucumber. Serve the falafels on top of the salad with 2 tbsp tzatziki dressing.

Day 7

BREAKFAST: Mango Sweet Rice

BASE
1/2 cup dry brown rice
1 cup frozen mango
3/4 cup water
2 chopped Medjool dates

ADD-ONS
1 tbsp coconut flakes
1 tbsp buckwheat groats

METHOD
Add water and rice into a small saucepan. Bring to a boil. Reduce heat to simmer and cover. Allow it to cook for 10 minutes. Add dates. Stir and let cook 25 more minutes or until all the water is absorbed. Pour rice with dates into a bowl and top with mango.

TIP: You can also make this in your rice cooker.

LUNCH: Curry Rice Bowl

BASE
1/2 cup dry brown rice
1/2 cup garbanzo beans
1 cup spinach
1 tsp curry powder
1 cup steamed vegetables
   (I like cauliflower, carrots and broccoli in this dish)

METHOD
Cook the dry brown rice as per instructions on the package. Place steamed rice, garbanzo beans, steamed veggies and spinach in a bowl. Add curry powder and mix well. Top with tzatziki or pre-made ketchup (from the meal prep section).

Day 7

DINNER: One Pot Pasta

BASE

1	12-ounce package gluten-free pasta
1	can (15oz or 443mL) chopped tomatoes
1	can (6oz or 178mL) tomato paste
2	cups water
1	tbsp Italian seasoning
1	tsp garlic powder
1	tsp onion powder
1	cup spinach
2	cups frozen veggies

ADD-ONS

1	tbsp nutritional yeast
~	Cracked black pepper
~	Fresh chopped basil

METHOD

Throw all the base ingredients into a large saucepan except the add-on toppings. Bring to a boil. Reduce heat to simmer and cook for about 10 minutes or until the pasta is al dente. Keep an eye on it. Depending on what pasta you use, the cooking times will differ. Refer to the cooking times on your package. Top with additional toppings if you wish. Have as much pasta as you desire for dinner. Save any leftovers for a quick lunch or snack or share this healthy meal with a loved one.

Week Two

Week Two Shopping Guide

STARCHES

1	1-pound bag of oats
1	2-pound bag brown rice
1	5-pound bag white potatoes
6	large sweet potatoes
1	package of 12 corn tortillas
1	1-pound bag muesli
1	15oz-can black beans
1	15oz-can salt-free pinto beans
1	1-pound bag dry red lentils
1	1-pound bag quinoa

VEGETABLES

1	1-pound box mixed greens
2	1-pound bags frozen corn
1	1-pound bag spinach fresh or frozen
2	white onions and 1 red one
2	15oz-cans chopped tomatoes
4	Roma tomatoes
1	tomato
2	6oz-cans tomato paste
1	stalk of celery
1	16-ounce bag frozen shredded hash browns
2	10-ounce bag frozen mixed veggies
2	medium zucchini
1	red pepper
1	cucumber
2	carrots
2	avocados
1	jalapeno
1	bunch cilantro
1	bunch scallions
1	garlic bulb
~	Add any other favorite veggies

FRUITS

1	16-ounce bag frozen mixed berries
1	15oz-can pineapple in juice
2	limes
5	bananas
1	mango or 1 1-pound bag frozen mango
2	lbs Medjool dates

SWEETNERS, SPICES, NUTS & SEEDS

Cinnamon

Cacao/cocoa powder

Cumin

Curry powder

Chili powder

Onion powder

Garlic powder

Ginger powder

Apple cider vinegar

Paprika

Sesame seeds

Oregano

1 can coconut milk

QUICK CONVERSIONS

1 pound = 454g

15oz = 443mL

6oz = 178mL

16 ounces = 1 pound

Week Two Meal Prep

Meal prep is instrumental for making your life a whole lot easier, especially if you have a job to go to every day and a family to cook for every night. This section will keep you sane during those busy times. If you do not want to do any meal prep and you have the time to cook all your meals fresh, feel free to skip this section.

THIS WEEK WE WILL PREP a few things in advance for breakfasts, lunches, and salads so when you are in a rush to get to work, you can quickly throw your breakfast and lunch together. Prepping your food ahead of time will also help keep you on track by having meals ready when hunger strikes or you are too tired to cook.

BAKED SWEET POTATOES
Preheat your oven to 450°F (232°C). Place 3 sweet potatoes on a baking sheet. Do not poke holes or make any cuts in them. Cook for about 35-45 minutes or until they are soft all the way through when pierced with a fork. Refrigerate for up to one week in an airtight container.

QUINOA
Mix 2 cups of dry quinoa and 5 cups of water and bring to a boil on your stove. Cover and reduce heat to simmer. Cook for 20 minutes. Refrigerate for up to one week in an airtight container.

BANANAS
It is always crucial to have at least 12 frozen bananas in your freezer at the beginning of the week. These are great for smoothies, banana milk, and nice cream. The best way to do this is always buy 12 extra bananas each week. Let them sit out until they get nice and spotty. Peel them and freeze them in either a large plastic container or a big freezer bag.

AVOCADO-CILANTRO DRESSING
1   avocado
1/2 lime, juice of
2   cloves garlic
1/2 cup fresh cilantro
1   jalapeno, deseeded
2   Medjool dates, soaked for one hour
1/2 tsp cumin
1/3 cup water

This sauce is used for dressings on salads as well as rice and bean bowls. You can also use it as a dip for veggies. Take all ingredients and blend on high in a blender. Refrigerate for up to one week in an airtight container. **LOW-SALT OPTION:** Add 1/4 tsp salt before mixing.

KETCHUP

1/2   cup water
1   6-ounce can tomato paste
4   Medjool dates, soaked in water for 1 hour
1   tbsp apple cider vinegar
1/4   tsp garlic powder
1/4   tsp dried oregano

If your dates are hard, soak them for 1 hour in the 1/2 cup of water then blend all the ingredients on high until smooth. Soft dates do not need to be soaked. Refrigerate for up to one week in an airtight container. **LOW-SALT OPTION:** Add 1/4 tsp salt before mixing.

CURRY-MANGO DRESSING

4   tbsp tahini or almond butter
6   dates, soaked in water for 1 hour
1/2   cup frozen mango
1   tsp curry powder
3/4   cup of water

If your dates are hard, soak them for 1 hour in the 3/4 cup of water then blend all the ingredients on high until smooth. Soft dates do not need to be soaked. Refrigerate for up to one week in an airtight container. **LOW-SALT OPTION:** Add 1/4 tsp salt before mixing.

PRE-MADE SALSA

4   Roma tomatoes
1/4   of a medium red onion
1/4   cup fresh cilantro
~   Juice of one lime

Chop your tomatoes, red onion, and cilantro into bite-sized pieces. Drizzle with lime juice. Refrigerate in an airtight container for up to one week.

REFRIED BEANS

1   can (15oz) salt free pinto beans
1   tsp chili powder
1   tsp garlic powder
1/2   tsp cumin
1/4   of a red onion, diced
~   Pinch of cilantro

Rinse your beans and add 1-2 tbsp water to your beans in a large bowl. Mash in spices, onion, and cilantro until smooth. You can also do this in your food processor. **LOW-SALT OPTION:** Add 1/4 tsp salt before mixing.

THAT'S IT FOR FOOD PREP THIS WEEK! Just spending an hour or two in the kitchen at the beginning of every week is worth the time you save cooking these things when you are starving or running out the door.

Day 8

BREAKFAST: Chocolate Oatmeal

BASE

1	cup dry oats
2	cups water
1	frozen banana, chopped
1	tbsp cacao or carob powder

ADD-ONS

1	tbsp coconut flakes
1	tbsp walnuts/nuts

METHOD

Combine oats, frozen banana, and water in a small saucepan. Bring to a boil. Reduce heat to low and cook 5 minutes or until all the water is absorbed. Stir occasionally. Add cocoa powder and mix. Add toppings.

LUNCH: Bean Tacos

BASE

4	corn tortillas (corn & water without flour on the ingredient list)
1	cup pre-made refried beans*
1/2	cup corn
1	cup steamed brown rice (1/3 cup dry)

ADD-ONS

~	Lettuce
~	Pre-made salsa*
~	Avocado dressing*

METHOD

Mix together refried beans, corn, and cooked brown rice. Spread mixture on each tortilla and top with lettuce, pico de gallo, and additional toppings.

Day 8

DINNER: *Dal & Rice*

BASE

1	cup dry red lentils
2	white potatoes, peeled and chopped
1/2	white onion, diced
1	carrot, chopped
2	garlic cloves, minced
1	can (15oz or 443mL) coconut milk
2	cups water
4	cups spinach
3	tbsp curry powder
1	tsp cayenne (optional)

METHOD

Add all ingredients except spinach into a medium-sized pot. Bring to a boil and reduce to simmer for about an hour or until lentils have soaked up all the water. About 5 minutes before serving, add spinach to pot and stir. Cook for a couple minutes. The dal is done. Enjoy 2 cups of dal over 1 cup of steamed brown rice.

Day 9

BREAKFAST: Muesli & Fruit

BASE
1   cup muesli
1   cup water
~   Sprinkle of cinnamon
2   cups of mixed berries

ADD-ONS
~   Coconut flakes
~   Buckwheat groats

METHOD
Bring 1 cup of water to a boil. Once the water comes to a boil, add muesli until soft. Combine muesli and fruit in a bowl. Top with cinnamon and enjoy!

LUNCH: Dal Salad

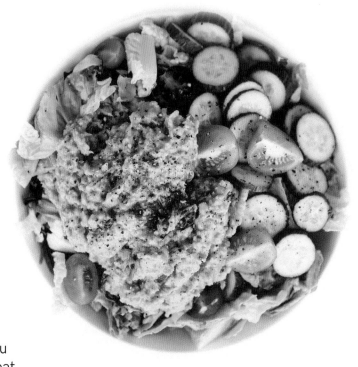

BASE
2   cups leftover dal
1   cup cooked brown rice (1/3 cup dry)
3   cups greens

ADD-ONS
1   tomato, diced
1/2 cucumber, chopped

METHOD
Place your greens, rice, tomato, and cucumber in a bowl. Top with leftover dal and additional toppings.

TIP: If you have a job outside of the home and want fresh cooked rice for your lunches, consider buying a small rice cooker for your office and bringing a bag of brown rice with you to work. It also can double as a crockpot to heat up leftover chili, stews, and soups for lunches.

Day 9

DINNER: *Curry Potato Fries*

BASE

3   medium potatoes, peeled
    and cut lengthwise into strips

1   tsp each, curry powder,
    garlic powder, onion powder

~   Pre-made ketchup*

METHOD

Preheat oven to 400°F (204°C). Cut and toss your fries in seasonings. Place the fries on a pan with parchment paper or directly on the rack (see video below for instructions). Bake for 30 minutes or until cooked through. Remove from oven. Dip in pre-made ketchup or whatever pre-made dressing you like.

https://highcarbhannah.co/recipes/crispy-potato-fries-no-oil/

Day 10

BREAKFAST: Potato Scramble

BASE
2   medium potatoes, chopped
1/4   white onion, chopped
1/3   red pepper, chopped
1   stalk celery, finely chopped
1/2   tsp each of garlic powder,
       chili powder, onion powder
1/2   cup water

ADD-ONS
~   Any other veggies you like
~   Nutritional yeast

METHOD
Place all ingredients in a shallow pan and bring to a boil. Cover with lid. Turn heat to low and cook until the potatoes are soft, about 10 minutes. Top with nutritional yeast and eat with pre-made ketchup.

LUNCH: Quinoa Sweet Potato Salad

BASE
1   cup cooked quinoa*
1   large sweet potato*
2   cups mixed veggies

ADD-ONS
~   Curry-mango dressing*
~   Sesame seeds

METHOD
Mix together your quinoa, sweet potato, and veggies in a large bowl. Pour the turmeric mango dressing over salad and add any additional toppings.

Day 10

DINNER: Garlic Mashed Potatoes

BASE

2	medium potatoes
2	medium zucchini
1	cup spinach
1/4	cup of the cooking water
Dash	of garlic powder, onion powder
~	Scallions

ADD-ONS

1	cup corn
2	cups steamed vegetables such as broccoli, cauliflower, asparagus, etc.
~	Nutritional yeast or black pepper

METHOD

Peel and chop your zucchini and potatoes. Fill a large pot with water and bring to a boil. Place potatoes and zucchini in pot and cover, bring heat down to a simmer and cook for 15-20 minutes or until soft. When potatoes are done, drain the majority of the water, leaving about 1/4 cup in the pot. Add your spices and mash the potatoes or use a hand blender to mix them until smooth. Place potatoes in a serving dish, top with corn, steamed vegetables, and nutritional yeast. Add fresh cracked black pepper to taste.

Day 11

BREAKFAST: *Overnight Oats*

BASE
1/2	cup dry oats
1	cups water
1/2	cup muesli
Dash	of cinnamon
~	Mixed berries

ADD-ONS
1	tbsp coconut flakes
1/4	cup mulberries

METHOD
Combine your oats, water and cinnamon in a jar and let sit in the fridge overnight. In the morning add muesli, and fill up the jar with any fruit you like and dash out the door. So easy!

LUNCH: *Mango Black Bean Salad*

BASE
2	cups greens
1/2	cup black beans, rinsed
1	cup cooked quinoa or rice*
1/2	mango, chopped/ 1/2 cup frozen
~	Avocado dressing*

ADD-ONS
~	Diced onion or chives
~	Sesame seeds
~	Corn tortillas

METHOD
Combine the greens, beans, quinoa in a bowl.
Chop up the mango and toss in a large bowl.
Top with the avocado dressing and any add ons.
Throw this mix in some corn tortillas and eat as a taco if you want something more than a salad.

Day 11

DINNER: Red Lentil Chili

BASE

1   cup dry red lentils
3   cups water
1/2 can (3oz) tomato paste
1   can (15oz or 443mL) diced tomatoes
4   Medjool dates
2/3 red pepper, chopped
1/2 white onion, chopped
1   tsp garlic powder
1   tbsp chili powder

METHOD

Add your red pepper, dates, tomato paste and water into your blender and blend until smooth. Add the red lentils and remaining ingredients into a large saucepan. Bring to a boil, reduce heat to simmer and cook for 30-45 minutes. Enjoy 2 cups of chili over 1 cup of steamed brown rice.

TIP: This is one of those recipes that tastes great as leftovers over warm rice for lunch at work. Add greens or other veggies to make it a totally different meal or eat with chopped avocado or hot sauce on top.

Day 12

BREAKFAST: *Sweet Potato Banana Bowl*

BASE
2   medium sweet potatoes*
1   banana, chopped
~   Sprinkle of cinnamon

ADD-ONS
1   tbsp ground flax seed
1   tbsp coconut flakes

METHOD
Chop up 2 of your already pre-cooked sweet potatoes and top with banana, syrup, and cinnamon.

LUNCH: *Chili Burrito Bowl*

BASE
1   cup steamed brown rice (1/3 cup dry)
1/2 cup corn
1   cup leftover red lentil chili
1/2 avocado

ADD-ONS
Leftover beans
Avocado dressing*

METHOD
Place steamed rice in a large bowl. Add corn, chili, and avocado. To get more greens in, use romaine leaves like a taco shell.

Day 12

DINNER: Tortilla Soup

BASE

1	1-pound package frozen organic corn
1	tsp garlic powder
1	tsp paprika
1	tsp chili powder
1	can (15oz or 443mL) tomatoes
6	corn tortillas chopped
3	cups water

METHOD

Combine all ingredients in a medium saucepan and bring to a boil. Lower heat and simmer for 10 minutes. Blend half the soup on high until creamy and add it back into the pot with the rest to cook another 5 minutes. Serve 2 cups of soup over 1 cup of steamed brown rice. Save any leftovers for lunch tomorrow.

Day 13

BREAKFAST: Chocolate Smoothie Bowl

BASE
2   frozen bananas
1   ripe banana
1   cup water
1   tbsp cocoa or carob powder

ADD-ONS
1   tbsp cacao nibs
1/4 cup muesli or oats
1 tbsp coconut flakes

METHOD
Blend frozen bananas, cocoa powder, and water until smooth. Place mixture in a medium-sized bowl. Add chopped fresh banana and any additional toppings.

LUNCH: Rice & Tortilla Soup

BASE
1   cup steamed brown rice (1/3 cup dry)
2   cups leftover tortilla soup
2   cups greens

ADD-ONS
~   Salsa
~   1/2 avocado
~   Leftover beans or quinoa

METHOD
Mix everything together in a medium-sized bowl. Top with your favorite toppings.

TIP: Use leftover tortillas to create tacos. Find creative ways to use up leftovers, and you will be surprised how much more diversity it will give your meals. The bonus is you won't have to throw away any spoiled food!

Day 13

DINNER: *Sushi Bowl*

BASE
2   cups steamed brown rice (2/3 cup dry)
1/2   avocado
1/2   cucumber, chopped
1   carrot, shredded
~   Sesame seeds
~   Nori sheets

METHOD
Combine all your ingredients in a bowl. Top with chopped nori and sesame seeds.

Day 14

BREAKFAST: Hash Brown Rounds

BASE
1 bag frozen hash browns
1 tsp garlic powder
1 tsp paprika
1 tsp onion powder
~ Cracked black pepper

METHOD
Preheat oven to 450°F (232°C). Defrost your hash browns. The easiest way is to take package out of freezer and put in the fridge the night before. The next morning or after your potatoes have defrosted, place potatoes and spices in a large mixing bowl and mix together. Use 1/2 cup of the mixture to form into a ball. Flatten ball until mixture resembles a patty. Repeat until the mixture is used up. You should get about 8 patties. Place the hash brown rounds on a baking sheet lined with parchment paper and bake 10 minutes. Flip and bake another 10 minutes or until they start to brown. Remove from the oven. Allow to cool before serving with ketchup.

LUNCH: Sweet Potato Fries

BASE
2-3 large sweet potato
~ Any pre-made dressing or your favorite dip*

METHOD
Preheat oven to 450°F (232°C). Cut your sweet potatoes into fries and toss with a pinch of salt. Place on a baking sheet lined with parchment paper or directly on the rack in the oven and bake for 35 minutes or until they start to brown. Eat with your favorite dip.

Day 14

DINNER: Veggie Stir Fry

BASE

2	cups steamed brown rice (2/3 cup dry)
2	cups of your favorite veggies
1	can (15oz or 443mL) pineapple
1	garlic clove, minced
1	tsp ginger powder

ADD-ONS

~	Fresh cilantro
~	Chopped scallions
1	tsp sesame seeds

METHOD

Stir fry the veggies in a shallow pan with the juice from the can of pineapples. Add the garlic clove and ginger. Sauté until veggies become soft. Add pineapple and cook another 2-3 minutes. Serve over rice and top with cilantro and scallions.

Going Forward

Congratulations! You finished all fourteen days of the LEAN & CLEAN lifestyle. Now what do you do? I know you won't reach your goals in fourteen days. This guide was written to give you a strong foundation of how to transition to a healthy eating plan. You now have the tools you need to be able to reach your goals in your own timeframe.

You will want to apply everything you have learned to reset your daily life. If you can follow the guidelines 100 percent, that is amazing, but that is not a reasonable expectation for many of you. We always have things that come up in our lives, friends who want to go out to eat, days when we don't want to exercise, travel, and so forth, but that doesn't have to get in the way of what you want to accomplish.

Do the best you can. Try to follow the principles in this guide as much as possible. For some of you that may be 95 percent of the time. Maybe you go out to eat once a week and have a meal with a little oil or salt in it. That is fine! One meal a week isn't going to sabotage your health or weight loss goals. You need to do what works for you! There were 53 recipes in this guide, and I hoped you found some you enjoy. Continue to eat those recipes. I also have an entire section on our website that I update frequently with recipes you can eat on this lifestyle.

If you are not already in the LEAN & CLEAN Facebook support group, you can join here: **https://www.facebook.com/groups/leanclean/**

Many members who have been extremely successful with this diet and lifestyle are willing to offer you support, new recipes, and inspiration. I am also there daily, and I would love to chat with you.

Remember: This is a journey. As long as you keep moving in the right direction, you will reach your goals. If you stray off course, know that it happens and there is a huge community here to support you and help you get back on track and stay there.

If there are any parts of the book that are unclear, please write me at support@highcarbhannah.co or ask in the LEAN & CLEAN facebook group. That way I can further update the book to be as clear and concise as possible.

Wishing you the very best on your journey,
Hannah

Nacho 'Cheese' Dip from
LET'S GET SAUCY

My Other Books

LET'S GET SAUCY

Over 55 mind blowing
vegan sauce recipes!

highcarb.co/saucy

WEIGHT LOSS
CHEAT SHEET

30 recipes + tons of info
to get you started!

highcarb.co/cheatsheet

INSTANT POT EBOOK

30 simple oil-free vegan pressure
cooker recipes for lazy f@cks.

highcarb.co/epic

PLANT APP

100s of recipes and customizable
meal plans right in your pocket.

highcarb.co/app

Printed in Great Britain
by Amazon

YOU CAN EAT HEALTHY
and have flavor too

HANNAH JANISH has been a plant based blogger for over 5 years. Going by High Carb Hannah on social media she runs a youtube channel with over 600k subscribers and has shared her journey of losing 70lbs through eating these delicious Whole Foods.

She continues to share delicious recipes, meal plans and her lifestyle to help inspire others to eat plants and not only help themselves get healthy and fit but also help the animals and our environment.

WEBSITE:
highcarbhannah.co

Cover Design: Jeannine Elder & Hannah Janish
Interior Design: Jeannine Elder (jeannine@potatoreset.com)
Photos: Hannah Janish

9 781949 950090